ANNA MANCINI

MAAT REVEALED

PHILOSOPHY OF JUSTICE IN ANCIENT EGYPT

BUENOS BOOKS AMERICA

ISBN: 1-932848-10-X (PAPERBACK) ENGLISH
ISBN: 1-932848-11-8 (E-BOOK) ENGLISH

English and Spanish versions published by:

BUENOS BOOKS AMERICA
bba@BuenosBooksAmerica.com
http://www.buenosbooksamerica.com

French version published by:
Buenos Books International (Paris)
www.BuenosBooks.com
BuenosBooks@BuenosBooks.com

FRENCH PAPERBACK: ISBN 2915495114
FRENCH E-BOOK: ISBN 2915495122
SPANISH PAPERBACK: 1-932848-06-1
SPANISH E-BOOK: 1-932848-07-X

CONTENTS

ACKNOWLEDGEMENTS

My deepest gratitude goes to:

Jacques BERCHON for his invaluable help during my research work at the Bibliothèque d'Egyptologie at the College de France

Gisèle PIÉRINI, from the Musée d'Archéologie Méditerranéenne in Marseille, for her kind welcome at the museum and for permission to take and use a picture of KHONSOU.MES' Coffin, (XXIst dynasty, inventory. 253)[1] for the cover of this book, and also for the permission to use the picture of Maat inside the book (Inventory 679) made by Yves GALLOIS for the museum.

The University Press of America, for their permission to publish a second edition of: Ancient Egyptian Wisdom for the Internet, UPA, ISBN: 0-7618-2378-6 in two different books: Maat Revealed, Philosophy of Justice in Ancient Egypt and Justice and Internet, a Philosophy of law for the virtual world. Both re-published by Buenos Books America.

Sources of the illustrations:

Drawing from the papyrus of Hunefer done by the author. (BM9900)

Picture of a statuette of Maat, by Yves Gallois for the Musée d'Archéologie Méditerranéenne in Marseille.

Cover: Picture of a detail from KHONSOU.MES' sarcophagus taken by the author at the Musée d'Archéologie Méditerranéenne in Marseille.

INTRODUCTION

ANCIENT EGYPT, A CIVILIZATION FOCUSED ON JUSTICE

The archeological remains of Egyptian civilization clearly prove that justice was essential to this people. Insofar as ancient Egypt was much more interested in justice than in law, it was a world very unlike ours. Egypt did not leave us a legal system as the Ancient Romans did,[1] but rather an idea of justice that our modern mentalities can hardly understand. Purely legal Egyptian archeological remains are very rare: only a few texts from the Late Period have been found. One of them, considered by Egyptologists to be the first international treaty, has reached us.[2] But the topic of justice can be found in the very acts of daily life. Almost all the texts and inscriptions discovered speak of justice. Egyptian justice deals not only with earthly life but also with the afterlife. Though the title of his book *La notion du droit d'après les Anciens Egyptiens (the idea of law according to the Ancient Egyptians)* Joseph SARRAF is also obliged to stress how essential the concept of justice was for this civilization and to highlight the scarcity of purely legal texts.[3] All the texts of wisdom teach that one has to conform to Maat, an unclear concept that Egyptologists have translated into the expression "Goddess of Truth and Justice". Through the ancient Egyptian *Book Of The Dead*, we know that justice is the measure by which the dead[4] will be judged when passing on and coming before the balance of Maat. This passing through the scales is shown in the illustrations called "vignettes" accompanying many funerary texts. As the passing through the balance of Maat appears to be a compulsory step before reaching the afterlife, it is easy to understand to what extent justice was an essential component of this ancient civilization which was so concerned about the afterlife. Therefore, the omnipresence of Maat, the Goddess of Truth and Justice, is not surprising. She appears in almost every text that Egyptologists have translated, such as texts of wisdom, funerary papyri, or hieroglyphic inscriptions carved on temple walls. Information on Maat was collected not only from the translation of texts but also from pictures.

Maat is the goddess with the white feather, the one who also holds an Ankh cross (symbol of life) in her hands. Through the remains of Egyptian civilization, we can easily understand that an Egyptian's whole life was governed by Maat. In such a world there is no difference between divine and human justice. The just man on Earth is also just in the afterlife. He is rewarded with lifely affluence, with prosperity in his earthly life as well as in his afterlife. Egypt as a "gift from the Nile" is marked by material prosperity which nevertheless did not stop it from striving for a high ideal of justice. But its concept of justice is so different from ours that the Egyptologists and the Historians of religions find it extremely hard to define it properly. As for modern legal researchers, amongst them there is very little interest in researching into the Egyptian concept of justice, which is generally completely ignored.

After having shown to what extent Ancient Egypt was a civilization focused on justice, we shall present the works of Egyptology and history of religions on Maat (Chapter 1). In Chapter 2, we shall see why the understanding of symbolic images is the best key to access this pre-logical world. In Chapter 3 we shall present how the specialists have taken poor advantage of the image of the scene of justice in the *Book of the Dead* and propose an in-depth interpretation of this symbolic image. This interpretation will allow us to actually understand this difficult concept. In Chapter 4, we shall present excerpts from Egyptian literature that confirm the symbolic meaning of the scene of justice from the *Books of the Dead* and our interpretation of Maat.

CHAPTER 1

MAAT THROUGH EGYPTOLOGY AND HISTORY OF RELIGIONS

1. Maat[5]: the Egyptian Goddess of Justice

On the basis of the information on the offering of Maat found in the temples, many experts portray Maat as the daughter of the sun god Ra,[6] as his mother[7] and also as his food and the food of all the gods. In his book entitled *Maât et Pharaon ou le destin de l'Egypte antique*, Jean-Claude GOYON depicts her as the daughter and the life of Ra.[8] The Egyptologists as well as the Historians of religions unanimously stress how essential Maat is to the Egyptian thinking. Indeed, Maat is the object of the most important ritual of exchange between the Pharaoh and the sun. This ritual consists in raising up Maat to her father the sun-god, that is to say to return to the sun the light he gives. Doing so will allow it to go on giving light for ever. This rite of exchange between the Pharaoh and the sun has recently been studied in detail by Emily TEETER[9] in a book entitled: *The Presentation Of Maat, Ritual And Legitimacy In Ancient Egypt*. Through her high interest in the observation of the pictures of the presentation of Maat by the Pharaoh or the king, found in temples, the author shows notably that Maat appears as the food of the sun[10] and also as the food of all the other gods. She writes:

> The royal presentation of Maat could be thought of as an archetypal offering, a supreme offering into which all other offerings are subsumed... This equation of Maat with other offerings is echoed in the epithet of Maat as 'food of the gods' and that the 'gods live on Maat.' She was considered to be the basic sustenance of the gods.

But what Maat does really mean? Her name is often rendered by the expression "Truth-Justice". What is the meaning of Maat painted on the walls of tombs and also appearing in the vignettes of the papyri as a goddess wearing a white feather on her head? She is also figured simply as a white feather, or by a statuette representing her, squatting with an Ankh cross (symbol of life) on her kneels.[11] Jean-Claude GOYON, for example, defines Maat as the universal order.[12] Such a definition is in conformity with the school of thought which abandoned the ethical conception of Maat, to consider Maat as a cosmic concept. We are now going to study the cosmic dimension of Maat.

2. From the ethical Maat to the cosmic Maat

Writings, found most of the time in tombs and temples, as well as hieroglyphs engraved in stone, were the main references out of which Egyptologists and Historians of religions have addressed the ancient Egyptian concept of Maat. They generally translated it into vague expressions like: "Truth-Justice", "Order" or "Truth".

Myriam LICHTHEIM wrote a book entitled *Maat In Egyptian Autobiographies And Related Studies,*[13] where she grouped references about Maat and made some commentaries. As a central concept of the Egyptian world Maat was of interest to Egyptologists as well as to Historians of religion.[14] However, as Egyptologists and

Historians of religions noticed, the many in-depth studies now available could never reach a clear understanding of this concept. They believe indeed that the lack of clarity concerning Maat comes from the difficulties for modern minds of entering ancient minds in order to understand them. So, if we want to have a sound understanding of the concept of Maat, we have to try to look at the Egyptian world with a neutral mind. We must also stop imposing our modern ideas of ethics or our modern way of reasoning. At the beginning, Egyptology did not escape the intellectual atmosphere of the nineteenth century. Hence it was inevitably influenced by the evolutionary theory and by scientific rationalism, which has been vividly criticized by Henri FRANKFORT. He advised trying to think in the ancient Egyptians' way, in order to understand their messages and the concept of Maat.[15] The school of thought having consisted in imposing on Maat our current conception of justice and in considering it as a purely ethical concept[16] - as the texts of the negative confessions found in tombs might allow us to believe- is today widely outdated, and the Egyptologists as well as the Historians of religions now consider Maat to be rather a cosmic concept. According to the Egyptologists Jan ASSMANN[17] and Philippe DERCHAIN, it is to Claas Jouco BLEEKER, (Dutch Historian of religions) that we owe, around the year 1929, the opening of this new horizon to Egyptology and history of religions. By this time scholars accessed a more global concept of Maat, a cosmic one. To reach such a result, Claas Jouco BLEEKER simply changed his viewpoint. We regret that the book he especially dedicated to Maat[18] is written in Dutch only. We could not find a translation of it in other languages and we had to work on the basis of quotations made by other writers able to read Dutch. Fortunately, BLEEKER, in a book written in English and published in 1967,[19] presents his views on Maat and above all the method that permitted him to reach a better understanding of the ancient Egyptian world. Claas Jouco BLEEKER reproached previous and contemporary searchers[20] for having taken a modern European viewpoint in the study of the ancient Egyptian religion. He criticized these scholars for having tried to find a religious doctrine in the ancient Egyptian literature, while in his opinion, such a doctrine could not exist in a world like Ancient Egypt. There people were not familiar with abstractions and dogmas. By the same token, he criticized the excessive and almost exclusive interest manifested by many researchers in the Egyptian mythology.[21] He explained that even the myth of Osiris has never been comprehensively presented by the ancient Egyptians themselves and that we owe the global presentation of this myth to the Greek author Plutarch.[22] The idea of creating a system logically structured, as well as the use of logical deductions, was very unfamiliar to the ancient Egyptian mind.[23] One of the main features of the Egyptian mind is its unfamiliarity with our modern rational way of thinking. Another important feature was a realistic and nature-oriented optimism that gave them the conviction of the immutability of Maat. Claas Jouco BLEEKER wrote:

> A note of optimism is struck by this conception of the fate of man. This optimism is characteristic of the view of life and the world held by the ancient Egyptian... the Ancient Egyptian lived in the unshakable faith that Ma-a-t, the order instituted by the sun-god in prehistoric

times, was, despite periods of chaos, injustice and immorality, absolute and eternal.[24]

In order to better understand the Egyptian religion (including the concept of Maat), Claas Jouco BLEEKER advised paying attention to rituals and cults, instead of focusing our attention on textual references. According to him, studying religious texts is a modern European attitude. In addition, he underlined that the retrieved Egyptian texts embody only the official religion and not the entirety of the beliefs and religious observances of the Egyptian people. The Egyptian people's ritualistic practices were, according to the author, much more varied than we could imagine through the sole approach of the official religion. Thanks to his enlarged approach which focused on the real ritual practices -within which the ritual of Maat was the most important-, which are actual acts of real life through which the Egyptians enacted their religious beliefs, Claas Jouco BLEEKER could demonstrate the cosmic dimension of Maat. He also showed how in the Egyptian world all was unified: social, and cosmic order, microcosm and macrocosm. He wrote:

> The ancient structure of this religion is most clearly shown in the conception of the goddess Ma-a-t. It can be said without any exaggeration that Ma-a-t constitutes the fundamental idea of ancient Egyptian religion. For Ma-a-t expresses the typically ancient view whereby the various fields of nature and culture - cosmic life, state policy, the cult, science, art, ethics and the private life of the individual- still form a unity.[25]

and gave the following definition of Maat:

> Ma-a-t is both a concept and a goddess. As a concept Ma-a-t represents truth, justice and order in corporate life, three ethical values which upon closer inspection prove to be based on the cosmic order.[26]

In his book, especially dedicated to Maat,[27] he presented his theory which served as a point of reference for many subsequent experts. Within them we can find Irène

SHIRUN-GRUMACH,[28] who on the basis of Claas Jouco BLEEKER's works stresses the idea that, as Maat is a cosmic symbol, the feather symbol that figures her represents the cosmic light. Jan ASSMANN also refers to the cosmic dimension of Maat, underlined by BLEEKER, to make a deeper study of this cosmic aspect of Maat. It is thanks to his intuition of the necessity of changing viewpoint as well as to his ability to observe reality that Claas Jouco BLEEKER made possible to open the horizons for a better understanding of the concept of Maat. He could have gone much further if he had applied to himself all the criticisms he addressed to the Historians of religions of his time. I.e. he reproached them for having adopted a European religious viewpoint in trying to understand the Egyptian religion. One could hardly ask BLEEKER, as an Historian of religions, to set aside history of religion, and also religion in order to better understand the concept of Maat.[29] Later on, some other experts have understood that the concept of Maat is not a religious one, in the general meaning we give today to the word "religion". Nowadays such a word implies the belief in something abstract which we cannot verify. Such a view was obviously alien to the very practical ancient Egyptian people. Philippe DERCHAIN could stress for example, to which extent the idea of order relating to Maat is not an abstract idea for the Egyptians but a real order resulting from opposing powers.[30] Regarding Maat, ancient Egyptians did not need to believe or not in it, they just had to experience it. They could do so, as many texts of wisdom advise them, through the observation of the variation of the results of their behaviors when opposing Maat or when in conformity with Maat.[31] Yet Claas Jouco BLEEKER wrote that contrary to our modern religions based upon texts, the Egyptian one was based upon nature.[32] He also concluded from a close observation of rituals and cults that they were all aimed at energy renewal,[33] thus it was a very practical and utilitarian kind of "religion". In thinking this, BLEEKER was in the same line as the former Egyptologist Alexandre MORET. This author had already underlined the practical side of the ritual of the offering of Maat, which consisted in the circulation of cosmic energy. Hence Maat, mainly involved in the flow of cosmic energy and in keeping the balance of the microcosm and macrocosm, does not appear to be a religious concept, in the meaning of the modern word "religious".

The Historian of religions, Henri FRANKFORT, was able to take sufficient distance from the modern religious approach to the Egyptian civilization and emphasized the "mythopoeic"[34] dimension of the Egyptian people.[35] In his book entitled *Ancient Egyptian Religion, An Interpretation*[36] he demonstrates how the Egyptian mind was very different from the modern mentality.[37] He believes that many Egyptian concepts, symbols and ideas seem obscure to us, not because the Egyptian sources are unclear, but only because we are confronted with a state of mind opposite to our own. The ancient Egyptians were not intellectual and cerebral people, they did not construct abstract logical theories and rational demonstrations. They were rather intuitive and pragmatic,[38] and they had a very rich imagination.[39] The author shows how, for example, our materialistic approach to the world hinders us from understanding for example, that while offering food to dead people or to gods, the Egyptians intended to offer the immaterial energy of this food. The Egyptians were not only interested in the material side of life, as we tend to be. They also took into account the immaterial. But it is very hard for modern people to understand that the Egyptians intended to offer to their gods the immaterial part of food:[40] that is to say its energy, which they called the "ka". Regarding the concept of Maat, FRANKFORT reckons that if this concept is so difficult to translate into our modern language, it is because it is related to a concept of life that is unfamiliar to us.[41] He believes this fact to be the main reason why we need so many unclear words to attempt translating this Egyptian concept, whereas this concept was a very unified one and reflected the unity between cosmic and social orders. Such a unity is also alien to our modern thinking.[42] According to FRANCKFORT, Maat is related to both ethics and morals, as well as to the human, divine or cosmic justice. He writes:

> But we lack words for conceptions which, like Maat, have ethical as well as metaphysical implications. We

must sometimes translate 'order', sometimes 'truth', sometime 'justice'; and the opposite of Maat requires a similar variety of renderings. In this manner we emphasize unwittingly the impossibility of translating Egyptian thoughts into modern language, for the distinctions which we cannot avoid making did not exist for the Egyptians.[43]

Taken in its cosmic dimension, Maat maintains the order of the world. But the word "order" should not be understood in its modern general meaning. According to FRANCKFORT the Egyptian meaning of "order" is unfamiliar to our modern minds. In the same way the word "right" does not have the same meaning as the modern meaning for "right". To be "righteous"[44] does not involve for the Egyptians any moral or ethical idea. Even if the Egyptians describe evil actions, they do not consider wrong behavior to be sins we should repent of. On the contrary wrong actions appear to them to be behavioral aberrations that impede human beings from being happy. The reason is that not conforming with Maat[45] brings disharmony and unhappiness. Pride for example, is considered to be the loss of the sense of proportion, as it was the case in the Greek conception of *hybris*.[46] A better understanding of Maat's functioning was consequently far more useful to the Egyptian people than uninstructed moral repentance from sins.[47]- Notwithstanding this feature of the ancient Egyptian mind, the author shows how under the fear of death and of the judgment of the dead, the late funerary Egyptian literature increasingly distorted the ancient Egyptian wisdom.[48] Regarding the idea of the judgment of the dead, the author believes that due to the Egyptian state of mind, this judgment could not have had the same ethical and moral meaning as the biblical one.[49] He criticizes the authors who believe they can draw the Egyptian morals or ethics from the funerary literature and from the topic of the judgment of the dead.[50] Strikingly, he asserts that this attitude is like attempting to draw modern astronomical knowledge from the horoscopes published in the newspapers.[51] On the contrary, many texts of wisdom prove that the concepts of sin, of ethics or morals were alien to the ancient Egyptians. Their minds were rather focused on the very practical cosmic balance permitted by Maat and its actual results in the microcosm as well as in the macrocosm.[52]

Finally, it is to the Egyptologist Jan ASSMANN that we owe one of the most recent in-depth studies of the concept of Maat.[53] Jan ASSMANN underlines the unity which is an essential feature of the Egyptian world and of the concept of Maat which concerns not only the cosmic but also the social life. Ancient Egypt, he explains "made no distinction between theology and science, cosmos and society".[54] Through a detailed analysis of the Egyptian texts and incidentally through the scene of the "weighing of the heart", the author demonstrates that Maat acts on a social as well as on a cosmic level. He believes that a sound understanding of the concept of Maat will be the key to understanding the Egyptian civilization.[55] He explains, as follows, how much the difficulties met in attempting to translate the concept of Maat are related to the opposition between our universe of thought and the Egyptians' one.[56] The author describes how Egyptology, enriched by cultural anthropology and the philosophy of civilization, evolved from a purely ethical conception of Maat to a cosmic one by the year 1930. Since then, Egyptologists have been considering that the heart of the concept of Maat was no longer ethics but the universal order.[57] Hence justice is the "action in conformity with the ruling forces playing a role in maintaining this universal order."[58]

The social dimension of Maat according to Jan ASSMANN[59]

Through an analysis of the texts of wisdom (composed of the instructions and the complaints) and especially of the text of the "peasant"[60] dated from the Middle Kingdom,[61] Jan ASSMANN attempts to demonstrate how the concept of Maat embodies the ideal of social solidarity. This active solidarity implies acting for the one who acts, and keeping the memory of yesterday. There is in addition solidarity of communication implied by the role played by hearing in the Egyptian civilization. Many criticisms can be formulated on this part of Jan ASSMANN's work which imposes on the Egyptian sources the modern and Christian oriented concepts of solidarity and altruism and also the modern approach to the hearing. Such concepts are assuredly alien to the Egyptian mind. The concept of hearing, for example, had in the Egyptian history a wider dimension that the "hearing-solidarity" described by JAN ASSMANN. Even if many texts emphasize the need for sons to "hear" their fathers,[62] this is assuredly a late distortion of the initial real meaning of the "hearing" which we can also find sometimes in the same Egyptian literature. In effect many texts deal with the "hearing of the gods" and with the "hearing of Maat" through the heart, which is quite different and of much more interest in the understanding of the ancient Egyptian mind. When hearing Maat through the heart, a man receives solar energy as well as the life force.[63] Let us recall that the modern science has discovered the essential role played by the ears as the organ of corporal balance. Doctor Alfred TOMATIS's works are also very informative when paralleled with the recent paleoanthropologists discoveries. Doctor Alfred TOMATIS writes:

> "Ears, in effect, were not initially conceived for hearing the sounds. How therefore can they listen? They must

ensure two major functions which are in reality one and the same thing: the balance and the energy recharge of the nervous system. It is only incidentally that ears will begin to hear and later on to listen".[64]

Paleoanthropologists found remains of primates without external auditory conduit. This now gives rise to a dispute among the experts as to whether these beings can be classified among the ancestors of human beings.[65] But let us come back to ancient Egypt and try to be aware of what hearing actually meant to the ancient Egyptians. In this way we will better understand why the concept of hearing was so essential within this civilization. Hearing was not limited to the human sphere, it was not "communication solidarity". Hearing extended to the cosmic order and implied being in tune with it, in order to fill the heart with Maat. Though Jan ASSMANN's works have the defect of imposing some modern moral values on the Egyptian world, they nevertheless contain some valuable aspects which deserve to be mentioned. The most important of them is the idea of exchange[66] associated with the idea of flow, of communication through exchanges. He demonstrates how the importance of exchange can be deduced from many Egyptian texts and especially through the sentence "act for who acts".[67] Hence we should only accept in part Jan ASSMANN's ideas and refuse his conclusion according to which we should abandon the idea that the cosmic order is central to the concept of Maat.[68] If according to Jan ASSMANN, we were to abandon the cosmic nature of Maat in favor of the concept of "communicative solidarity", we would regress considerably and lose in doing so the benefit of the progress made possible by Claas Jouco BLEEKER. This would also result in considerably narrowing and obscuring the concept of Maat by imposing modern concepts on it. Nevertheless the importance of exchanges emphasized by Jan ASSMANN must be retained. We can keep this without abandoning the cosmic approach to Maat. This law of exchange has also been underlined by S. BICKEL[69] in his book entitled: *La cosmogonie égyptienne avant le Nouvel Empire*. Insofar as Maat is involved in all kinds of exchanges, human as well as cosmic, it is through a balanced exchange (human or cosmic) that the flow of solar energy is well maintained. In such a context, there is no "solidarity" in the modern meaning, but only a realistic approach to the law of the circulation of Maat with the aim of creating harmony, affluence, and good health.

In conclusion, through the evolution of thought on the concept of Maat, it appears that Maat is very different from our modern concepts of truth, hearing, solidarity, sin, etc... It is probably a remote ancestor of our modern concepts. Due to these facts we can only reject Bernadette MENU's positivistic approach to the study of the link between Maat, Thot of Hermopolis and the law.[70] According to the author, Maat is the divine norm and Thot is in charge of the application and interpretation of the divine norm.[71] To "say Maat" means "to say the law", "to create the case law". Such a view is perfectly modern. Far from this positivistic platitude a specific and original concept of justice stems from the ancient Egyptian world. Maat is completely different from our idea of justice which is mainly focused on the material world. On the contrary the main focus of the Egyptian justice is the immaterial world of life energy.

However, even though a great amount of information on Maat is available, this concept still remains too unclear. We have to go on searching for the real meaning of Maat. For this purpose we must try to forget our modern universe of thought in order to go further away into the ancient Egyptian mentality. The symbol is one of the gates that can open the way. Let us speak about the role played by symbols in ancient Egypt.

CHAPTER 2

SYMBOLS AS A KEY TO ACCESS A PRE-LOGICAL WORLD

Through the study of the concept of Maat, we are able to notice the modern bias which has consisted in studying Maat mainly through written sources to the detriment of pictures. A famous Egyptian picture named by the scholars "the weighing of the heart" or "The judgment of the Dead" appears to be of great value for the understanding of the concept of Maat. This picture, endlessly reproduced, is unique in portraying Maat in action. Before speaking of the very poor advantage Egyptology and history of religions have taken from this essential picture, it is important to understand what the symbols were to the Ancient Egyptian people.

1. Ancient Egypt: a world of symbolic communication

Ancient Egypt was so focused on justice that there is a

wealth of references to Maat. What is lacking is only our ability to understand them, mainly because we have a foible for texts and a tendency to ignore symbols and pictures. Being aware of the importance of symbols as means of communication in ancient Egypt will allow a better understanding of the ancient Egyptian concept of justice. We will be then able to rebuild, thanks to the pictures which complement the discovered texts, a precise, unified, and purposeful definition of what justice was to the ancient Egyptians. The ancient Egyptians' thinking has been portrayed as "pre-logical", "pre-philosophical", "pre-classical", or simply "simple"[72] in comparison with that of the axial era[73] which stemmed from the ancient Greek rational way of thinking. In an article called "La pensée préphilosophique en Egypte", the Egyptologist Jean YOYOTTE[74] falls into line with the usual opinion of scholars, when he demonstrates that the ancient Egyptians did not invent rationally and logically constructed systems.[75] The author also underlines the fact that Egypt did not know a legal logic similar to the modern one.[76] We have only to glance at their imaginative hieroglyphic writing, and at their often humorous way of depicting reality, to understand to what extent our rather cold and abstract logical rationality was alien to them. In their pictorial universe, full of colors, life, and imagination, we can see snakes with legs, winged eyes or eyes with two legs, which were used to indicate the movement.[77] There are also many colored birds, more than 80 different kinds during the pre-ptolemaic era, according to Erik HORNUNG, who asserts that writers in the Middle Ages called the hieroglyphs "the writing of birds".[78]

The ancient Egyptians' privileged means of communication were the symbols[79] they considered to contain a life force.[80] This last point appeared so real to them that from a certain era they used to mutilate, on the walls of the tombs, the symbols portraying animals and human beings to prevent their aggression towards the deceased.[81] As Erik IVERSEN[82] underlines, designs were firstly living things with magical powers. More generally speaking, regarding the artistic works of Egypt he stresses their primary visual role. He writes:[83]

> The meaning of each individual representation could only be visually conceived and could never be expressed in any fixed or established sequence of words or sentences, but each of them had nevertheless a specific message to convey, and a definite event or sequence of events to describe or enact.

Nowadays we are used to approaching signs only with our rational mind. Most of us have lost the capacity to properly understand symbols and modern man has simply lost the meaning of his own dream language. However it is through dreams that we come closer to the symbolic way ancient civilizations used to communicate through images. Egyptologists are not trained to understand dream language either. This means that even the most gifted specialists have no chance of understanding the messages conveyed by the ancient Egyptian images when they are not even able to understand their own dream language. Conversely, if Egyptologists were properly trained to understand their own dream language, great progress would be achieved in the field of Egyptology. Ancient Egyptian symbols like dream language convey a deep meaning which cannot be reached by the modern mind alone.

But symbols are rich in meanings. As Beatrice L. GOFF notices, the symbol, contrary to the "sign", means much more than what it portrays. The symbol can portray ideas, emotions, intuitions as well as experiences.[84] Symbols can be compared to compressed computer files needing to be expanded[85] by the use of specific skills. Hence the use the ancient Egyptians made of symbols to convey their secret and sacred knowledge. Another possibility offered by the symbol is that it permits multi-level communication according to the ability of the person who looks at it. A symbol can deliver a lot of valuable information to a sensitive and intuitive person, while the same symbol will tell nothing to somebody unable to look at it, but prompt to impose on it his preconceived ideas. Today, the main obstacle to our understanding of ancient Egyptian symbols is definitely our tendency to impose on them our preconceived ideas as well as our way of reasoning. The ability to approach the symbols impartially can be named the internal silence.[86] This silence, which permits us to receive the real message of the Egyptian symbols, is something cruelly lacking, especially to the educated and learned people that Egyptologists and Historians of religions usually are. Instead of simply watching the picture without *a priori*, they have wrongly labeled "the weighing of the heart" or "the judgment of the Dead", they unfortunately let the "magic" funerary texts accompanying this picture completely divert their attention. But the funerary literature is not, as many experts have demonstrated, a reliable reference in order to understand the Egyptian philosophy of life and the meaning of the concept of Maat. Another modern foible to be added to the lack of "mind silence" is that we are indeed very narrow minded when we imagine that only our modern civilization has a scientific knowledge and the only correct way to express it: the scientific language. Nevertheless, a few Egyptologists have made the hypothesis that the ancient Egyptians used symbols as means for scientific communication, i.e. to convey scientific knowledge.[87]

2. Science and symbolic communication in Egypt

As we already mentioned, Maat has been translated by "Truth", "Justice", "Order", "light", "food of the gods", and as Jan ASSMANN[88] writes, the paraphrase or the enumeration could end in forming an entire book. Even if we were able to find the exact definition of Maat, the situation would not be much improved. In this context, what matters is not finding out an abstract definition of Maat but to understand the practical functioning of Maat. Such an understanding makes necessary a scientific observation of Maat. In other words, a sound observation of the reality embodied in the picture must prevail over a religious approach, a moral one or one which is only descriptive or archeological. Only a scientific approach to Maat will enable us to find a unity between all the many aspects of Maat studied by Egyptologists and Historians of religions. But the scientific meaning of the picture of the "weighing of the heart" cannot be discovered through the use of our scientific traditional thinking. The main reason is that Egyptian scientific knowledge was embodied in symbols.

Today scientists do not pay any kind of attention to symbols, which appear to them to be negligible things. Nevertheless, some experts have questioned themselves on the possibility of a scientific approach to the highly symbol-oriented Egyptian civilization. They have underlined the scientific side of certain elements of the Egyptian civilization. Siegfried MORENZ asserted that Egypt had a scientific and mythic writing and that in this civilization science and religion were intermingled. He believed that without being rational as we are, the ancient Egyptians expressed their scientific knowledge in a mythical language.[89] According to him, in ancient Egypt scientific knowledge was religious knowledge. Philippe DERCHAIN did not share this opinion. Broadly speaking, he thought to the contrary that religion was science. Philippe DERCHAIN, to whom we owe an excellent translation of the Papyrus Salt[90] on the ritual for life conservation in the ptolemaic Egypt, stresses the scientific aspect of what according to him we wrongly call "Egyptian religion". The author is in the same line of though as Alexandre PIANKOFF[91] that he quotes when considering that there was not a religion in Egypt but a system of physics.[92] Philippe DERCHAIN reached the conclusion that there is no actual Egyptian religion in the modern sense.[93] We can also find in this author's work one of the most energy-oriented approaches to the Egyptian civilization. Going further than many experts he did not hesitate[94] to compare, in the same way as Serge SAUNERON[95] did, the Egyptian temple to an electric power station. Jean-Claude GOYON has also in another context stressed the role played by temples as collectors of life energy.[96] But Philippe DERCHAIN followed through the energetic logic of temples when he also explained that the Egyptian gods appeared to be points of emergence[97] of natural powers, stimulated through specific rituals.[98] Gods for example must be regularly recharged[99] in the temples.

One cannot deny the Egyptians' interest in the energy side of the cosmos and of the human group. Such an interest was manifest through their focus on the sun and on solar energy flow, also called Maat. As a closer observation of the scene of the "weighing of the heart" will reveal, the ancient Egyptians were interested in the circulation law of solar energy through the cosmos and among the human beings. But insofar as the majority of ancient Egyptian documents are vitiated by a jumble of superstitions and magic, we must carefully select among them the most valuable information. As an example, even if we share Philippe DERCHAIN's opinion according to which the Egyptian temple could be compared to a power station, we cannot admit that the Egyptian rituals are thoroughly scientific. The rituals, like the Egyptian literature, reached us vitiated and distorted in the course of the very long Egyptian history by a jumble of non scientific practices, and of religious constraints. How can we still recognize an Egyptian scientific knowledge through the description of the daily cult made by Jean-Claude GOYON[100] where the statue of the god was fed, dressed, arrayed like a human?

The ritual indeed seems to erase by many aspects the energetic aim for which it was probably originally established. The huge contradiction between the Egyptians' interest in solar energy and the rigidity of these rituals makes obvious that they[101] contain only a slight and distorted souvenir of a remote knowledge. According to Philippe DERCHAIN, the aim of the ritual described in the papyrus SALT, of which the instructions had to be obeyed to the letter, was to maintain the cosmic order.[102]

In conclusion, the information we should retain is mainly the energy aspect of the Egyptian concept of justice. The permanence of this essential concept within their civilization clearly demonstrates the Egyptians' interest in the immaterial side of life: the human and cosmic energy. Such an energy-oriented concept of justice could hardly have been translated in a simple way into a modern language. Which, invented by modern minds, is mainly focused on the materialistic side of life. What do a justice dedicated to life energy and a justice dedicated to matter have in common? The aim of Egyptian justice was to allow a correct flow of the very rich solar energy. To them, this was a way to create abundance, prosperity and health for all, while the justice of the material world deals mainly with sharing a limited amount of things. Hence, such a justice does not aim to create prosperity but only to manage what already exists in a limited amount. It is only very recently that the famous psychologist Karl Gustav JUNG spoke of psychic energy,[103] though it appears from the ancient Egyptian documents, that these people were focused on the energy side of life,[104] on the cosmic as well as on earthly levels. This very side of life is to a wide extent ignored today. Hence it is not surprising that when embracing the Egyptian civilization with materialistic modern eyes, we are unable to access the scientific messages embodied in some Egyptian archeological remains like the scene of the "weighing of the heart". A greater interest in the forces of life would facilitate a sound understanding of the Egyptian world. Unfortunately, this is precisely what our modern legal philosophy seems to have forgotten. An approach to the concept of Maat through energy is indeed a privileged way to better understand the Egyptian mind. Maat is a key concept and if we can really understand it, we shall be able to answer many other unresolved questions about the Egyptian civilization.

CHAPTER 3

A SCENE OF JUSTICE IN THE *BOOK OF THE DEAD*

(Drawing from the papyrus of Hunefer (BM9900) done by the author.
Original image available online:

www.siloam.net/rostau/ newgiza/entrance.html;

www.guardians.net/hawass/ tomb_of_iuf-aa.htm;

http://web.ukonline.co.uk/gavin.egypt.)

The scene named "the weighing of the heart" or "the judgment of the Dead", which portrays Maat in action, has been conveyed mainly through the funeral literature contained in the *Ancient Egyptian Book Of The Dead*.

Hence as a prerequisite to the presentation of how Egyptologists and Historians of religions viewed the scene of the "weighing of the heart" (we shall call from now the SCENE for sake of convenience) we must explain what is the *Book Of The Dead*.

1. What is the *Ancient Egyptian Book Of The Dead*?

Contrary to what one might assume the *Ancient Egyptian Book Of The Dead* is not a unique book. This "label" was attributed by the experts to a funerary literature composed of a number of scattered spells which were compiled and divided into Chapters. The actual Egyptian title given to this compilation is according to the authors the *Book Of Coming Forth By Day*.[105] Guy RACHET reminds us that CHAMPOLLION chose the title *Funeral Ritu*al when publishing one of these compilations. According to Guy RACHET, the German Egyptologist Karl Richard LEPSIUS invented the title *Todtenbuch* (*Book Of The Dead*) and the division into chapters.[106]

Hence, the division into Chapters was arbitrary, as Guy

RACHET underlines. As for Jean YOYOTTE, he considers the *Books of the dead* to be a compendium of unrelated incantations.[107] According to him the SCENE was initially accompanying both chapter 30 on the heart and chapter 125 on the declaration of innocence. But in later versions of the book, the SCENE appears only with chapter 125 where the scene and the judgment seem to have been merged.[108] There are lots of variations in the details of the SCENE from one book to another, as Jean YOYOTTE asserts. He also emphasizes the heterogeneous composition of this SCENE[109] in the most recent versions of the *Book Of The Dead*. Despite the many translations effected by experts the *Book Of The Dead* still remains obscure. One of the reason is that it is strongly tinted by a magic of which the aim is to help the deceased to pass successfully to the next world. This magic is also intended to help counter the addition of obstacles met on the way. Such a rise in dangers were the result of[110] the increasing fear of death as Egyptian history progressed, correlating with the increase of religious power. Both made the obstacles multiply and become more and more terrifying. With Chapter 125, called by Egyptologists

"Declaration of innocence" or "Negative confession", the deceased had to have a magic spell performed to have his innocence magically declared and this, apparently, independently from his actual moral behavior. Chapter 30A is in the same register and its title is: "For not letting N's heart create opposition against him in the realm of the Dead".[111] The magic which erases the breaches of morals specific to the time where the books were written is so much present in these texts that one could accuse the ancient Egyptians of pharisaism. As Etienne DRIOTON noticed, on the basis of the Texts of Wisdom, the *Book Of The Dead* did not reflect the state of mind of the whole Egyptian people.[112] Its many magic words, its heterogeneous composition, sometimes the lack of link between the text and some details of the vignettes,[113] the fact that the SCENE has been simultaneously linked with the chapter 30 on the heart and with chapter 125 on the declaration of innocence,[114] all this results in making the *Ancient Egyptian Book Of The Dead* a poorly reliable written reference. Nevertheless the Egyptologists and Historians of religions reckon that they cannot prevent themselves from describing the SCENE without reference to Chapter 125 and hence to the ideas of judgment, punishment, sin, and so on which these implied. Jean YOYOTTE, who wrote an in-depth study on the judgment of the dead, where he made the following very interesting hypothesis, does not himself escape this foible. Taking into account the most ancient pictures of the SCENE as well as the chapter 30B, the author assumes that the SCENE was initially separate from the scene of the court trial and that these two scenes later merged in one scene.[115] His research was more historical than philosophical. He aimed mainly at determining when the idea of the judgment by god appeared in Egypt. For this reason, he did not draw the consequences of his interesting assumption. He mainly used texts analysis and statistics which are very modern and academic ways to access information. They ignore completely the other possibilities of accessing information which were used by preference by "primitive people". Even though traditional methodology has been able to produce some remarkable results in Egyptology and in History of religions, one must regret the lack of interest in pictures and symbols it involves. It is indeed through the pictures engraved in stones or painted on walls and on papyri that Egypt transmitted its most permanent messages. It is also thanks to pictures that our modern minds, used to bringing too much rationality to the study of texts, have the opportunity of changing this deep-rooted habit. Pictures can allow a more spontaneous feeling, closer to the pre-logical mind of the ancient Egyptian world. As we can see through their descriptions of the SCENE, experts have not been able to escape the hold of the writings in order to perceive the whole message which a symbolic picture conveys. Even Erik HORNUNG, who advocates a greater consideration for the picture in Egyptology, falls into the trap of a too intellectual and not sufficiently sensitive modernity. In the first chapter of his book: *L'Esprit du temps des Pharaons*, Erik HORNUNG considers that a picture (hieroglyphic or not) is, as much as a word, a key to understand the Egyptian world.[116] He describes how the use of different colors in pictures and hieroglyphs implies specific meanings.[117] Regarding the debates around Rameses II, the author regrets the little consideration we have for ancient Egyptian pictures.[118] He believes that texts are not enough, we must decipher the pictures.[119] Unfortunately he did not make the most of his remarkable awareness of the importance of Egyptian iconography while studying Maat.[120] Like many other scholars, he did not pay enough attention to the picture showing Maat in action. He contented himself with a superficial description, under strong influence of the funerary literature. In summary, due to its heterogeneous structures and its magical aims, The *Ancient Egyptian Book Of The Dead*, does not appear to be the best means to understand the SCENE. It would be better to look at the SCENE itself, without reference to this unreliable funerary literature, but keeping in mind how important communication through symbols and pictures was for the Egyptians. The ancient Egyptians considered that drawings and writing were sacred.[121] The knowledge they conveyed was not offered to all.[122] Far from being free in their creations, the artists had to follow strict religious rules and to work under the control of priests.[123] Due to the specific feature of the ancient Egyptians' mind, it is necessary to give to the SCENE the full attention it deserves. It is through this unique picture -endlessly reproduced- showing Maat in action, that we have the best possibility of finding the valuable information about the concept of Maat. That is to say the least distorted by priests and magicians,[124] the most permanent information and the least altered by the cultural changes which occurred in the long history of Egypt. Focused on the funerary texts, the Egyptologists and the Historians of religions did not make the most of the symbolic representation of justice in action. They were too much under the influence of the context of death and could not see the picture with their eyes. As an example of method, opposite to the pre-logical mind of ancient Egyptians, we can mention Jan ASSMANN's view on the method he used to try to understand Maat, which essentially focused on the discourses in which Maat is central.[125] (Nevertheless, the author does, incidentally, describe the SCENE). As for Jean YOYOTTE, it is with a definitely scientific mind that he approaches the concept of Maat through advising a statistical study of the sources.[126]

2. The SCENE from the angle of scholars

We are now going to present below some examples of the Egyptologists and Historians of religions' views of the SCENE, which is indifferently named: "the judgment of the dead" or "the weighing of the heart". In his book entitled *le Nil et la civilization égyptienne,* Alexandre MORET perceives the SCENE mainly as a court trial. In an article dedicated to the doctrine of Maat,[127] the author describes the texts and completely omits the picture. In another more specific article on the judgment of the dead, we can find a description of the SCENE as a court, before which the heart is weighed against Maat.[128] As for Jean YOYOTTE, he has written one of the most in-depth articles on this topic[129] where he also tries to determine when and how the idea of the judgment of the deceased by god appeared in Egypt. He describes the SCENE as a weighing of the heart before a court. Jan ASSMANN[130] has written one of the most recent books dedicated to the concept of Maat. In his chapter on the afterlife and immortality he describes the SCENE with the help of the texts of the *Book Of The Dead.* He underlines the fact that the SCENE conveys the idea of a transition between two worlds.[131] He considers that this transition is pictured through the use of the idea of a divine tribunal.[132] He explains how the "ba" figured as a bird is linked to the idea of transition. The "ba" is symbolically figured as a bird which through flying operates the transition between the Earth and the sky. He concludes that the "ba" is a concept symbolizing the transition between the visible and the invisible.[133] His analysis is mainly based upon the New Empire definitive texts of chapters 30 and 250 of the *Book Of The Dead*, that is to say relatively recent texts, tinted with so much magic, and where the concept of Maat has faded. Jan ASSMANN makes a very brief description of the SCENE. He believes this judgment to be a rite of initiation[134] intended to judge as well as to purify the deceased from his sins as expressed by the title of chapter 125.[135] He describes the SCENE mainly as a weighing of the heart where when the heart is made heavy with sins, the deceased is found guilty.[136] We are now going to quote extensively from two descriptions of the SCENE.

2. 1: R.O. FAULKNER's description of the SCENE

The author writes the following description of the vignette from the papyrus of HUNEFER (British Museum 9901/3):

> Anubis introduces Hunefer to the Weighing of his Heart against the feather of Maat. Anubis, depicted a second time, checks the accuracy of the balance; Thoth stands ready to write down the result, watched by the monster Ammit, who gobbles down hearts laden with sin. Vindicated, Hunefer is introduced by falcon-headed Horus-avenger-of-his-father to Osiris, who is enthroned in an elaborate booth with Isis and Nephthus behind him and the Four Sons of Horus standing on a lotus before. Above, behind an offering-table and adored by Hunefer, squat fourteen gods and goddesses who are witnesses to the judgement.[137]

2. 2: Siegfried MORENZ's description of the SCENE

In his book entitled *Egyptian Religion*, Siegfried MORENZ[138] studied the concept of Maat. In this context he described the SCENE and underlined the fact that Maat is the "measure of judgment upon men". He explained that due to the magical nature of chapter 125 of the *Book Of The Dead*[139] and to the fact that these texts do not refer to any effective hearing of the deceased,[140] he based his description on the vignette of the "judgment of the dead" to try to understand the concept of Maat. He describes the vignette as a scene showing a court in charge of the ethical judgment of the deceased. Here follows his description of the vignette illustrating chapter 125 of the *Book Of The Dead*:

> Here the vignettes accompanying the text (the details of which vary) show that the dead man's heart, deemed to be the seat of the intellect and will as well as the life-giving center of the physical body, is weighed against the symbol of Maat (usually depicted as a feather), which serves as an ethical standard. Anubis.... is master of the balance, and is in control of the pointer; the scribe Thoth records the verdict and announces it. If the verdict should be unfavorable, the sinner falls victim to 'the devourer'.... a hybrid monster with the head and jaw of a crocodile."..[141].

We can notice at once that the author did not really look at the picture, but simply imposed on it the modern ideas of ethics, sin, and judgment. But we have to recognize his merit in pointing out that we should pay more attention to the picture, in this context more reliable than texts.

3. An actual observation of the SCENE

3. 1: Criticism of the method used by scholars

Having explained how scholars depicted the SCENE, we can now address the following criticisms of their approach. First, the titles they choose to label the SCENE: "The judgment of the dead" or "The weighing of the heart" unfortunately narrow the scope of the reflection. We all know the influence of titles on our brain. In this occurrence they have kept the scholars' brain focused on the ideas of judgment, of death, of ethics, of measure of the souls, etc... If we really look at the picture, where can we see a corpse? How can we pretend that there is a judgment in the modern meaning? The god contents himself with recording a result.

The supposedly dead is pictured very alive. The whole scene, where Maat is figured as a feather and on the top of the scales, suggests life more than death. Isn't Maat the opposite of death? The SCENE, in fact seems to picture a life process, as we shall explain in more detail, and does not deal with death and judgment at all. A second main mistake made by the experts has consisted in imposing on this very ancient picture our modern conceptions of conscience, purity, ethics. Assuredly such concepts began to appear in the late history of Egypt, but how can we reasonably see them in the SCENE? Such an ethical approach to the SCENE is too abstract in comparison with the ancient Egyptians' very practical mind. It is a great mistake to impose on this picture, and especially onto the drawing of the heart, our modern ethical concepts. Regarding the heart, provided we remain as practical as the ancient Egyptians were, there is much more to understand through the SCENE. Besides, the scholars had a modern approach and too materialistic to the scales. The idea that the pair of scales is actually weighing a heart against a feather is very materialistic and moreover unreasonable on the same materialistic ground. Let us remember that prior to being a device for a physical weighing, the pair of scales is the symbol for the act of exchanging physical or intangible things. In other words, **exchanging** and not weighing is the main thing. How would it then be possible to understand from the materialistic point of view this Egyptian advice addressed to a man "You must be like the scales"?[142] Insofar as the pair of scales has been for ages a device used to weight material things for commercial purposes, the scholars have naturally imposed on the picture the idea of a weighing. Also, the pair of scales has always been the symbol of exchange, of a balanced exchange and of justice. The pair of scales is also the symbol of the cosmic balance and this has nothing to do with weighing. An Egyptian text advises: "don't lie, you must be a balance".[143] Our materialistic approach to the scales cannot permit a correct understanding of this Egyptian literature. Anyway, if you look at the SCENE closely, you will soon be obliged to admit that it cannot reasonably picture a weighing. In the following section we shall actually describe the SCENE without (as much as it is possible) imposing on it our modern ideas and above all without being seduced by the funerary literature. This is crucial insofar as Henri FRANKFORT has explained that this kind of literature, so tinted with fear, is unreliable.[144] He has also vividly criticized the scholars who believed they could deduce from the judgment of the dead the ancient Egyptians' ethical preoccupations. According to Henri FRANKFORT, this literature should not be considered so highly.[145] Taking into account the relevant observations made by Henri FRANKFORT, we are now going to describe one of the most famous presentations of Maat in action. We shall exclude the funerary literature initially, while after we shall sift out of it the valuable information it contains regarding the functioning of the heart in connection with Maat.

3. 2: Description of the SCENE

The scene we are going to describe comes from a vignette found in the *Book Of The Dead* of HUNEFER, an Egyptian man who lived around 1310 B.C. This scene has been very often reproduced in part or in whole in many books dedicated to ancient Egypt. It is very famous.

We can see in this picture a man dressed in white (the scholars say this is the way Egyptian people used to portray the deceased)[146] giving his hand to an animal headed being holding an Ankh,[147] who leads him. These two characters are coming to a pair of scales, of which the central position in the picture strongly catches the eye. We shall later describe it in more detail. Under the scales we can see the same being (the god Anubis), seated, adjusting the scales, and also an heterogeneous animal (called in Egyptology: "The great devourer" or Ammit).[148] The body of this animal faces the man in white, while with the head turned backwards it is looking at the man in white passing by. The two representations of the god Anubis -once leading the man in white by the hand, then seated adjusting the scales-in addition to the movement backwards of the Great Devourer's head, render the idea of movement, of passage. The man in white, has moved, he has circulated. The SCENE suggests a link between balance of the scales and the circulation. Contrarily a link would exist between the scales' imbalance and the obstruction of the way, probably pictured by this monster-looking animal. An Ibis-headed god, Thot, records the result of the scales. Hence, we can deduce that no judgment in the modern meaning occurs. There are no court and judges making a decision but only a pair of scales. Scales always tell the truth without a need for a judgment by man or god. It is a natural law that is being portrayed. It is striking that it is the pair of scales, standing in the middle of the SCENE, which decides how the story will continue. Thanks to this precise and mechanical device, which does not allow treachery,[149] the way will be open or not to the man in white. This is the reason why the pair of scales is the instrument of Truth, it cannot lie, and we can notice on the top of it the head of Maat (in some other pictures only the feather). The pair of scales involves the natural and automatic functioning of a natural law. Another bird headed character[150] holding an Ankh, symbol of life, opens to the man in white, with a movement of his hand, the way towards Osiris enthroned and ready to welcome him.

In the middle of the picture, the pair of scales, with two pans on the same level, portrays Maat in action. In the papyrus of HUNEFER, the goddess Maat's head appears at the top of the scales and Maat is also present on one of the pans as a white feather. The central theme of the scales associated with the goddess Maat -in the different books, the theme varies only regarding a few details-[151] appears to give the most valuable information on Maat. Let us have a closer look at the scales. What is there on each pan? What is really happening? In doing so let us try to be as practical and as close to nature as the ancient Egyptians were. On one of the pans we can see the drawing of the vase the Egyptian used to diagram a heart.[152] On the other pan there is the white feather representing the goddess Maat. If we observe the action taking place in a realistic way, we must reckon that:

1°) On a practical point of view: a feather on one side and a heart in a vase on the other side cannot -if they were really weighed- result in balancing the scales.[153] Hence this picture cannot portray any weighing in the material meaning.

2°) On an abstract point of view: a human being even with an excellent heart cannot make the weight against a goddess. Hence, even in abstraction there is no possible weighing of a heart.

The SCENE is for something else. The objects on the pans are very tiny in comparison with the dimension of the scales, which makes the balance of the scales more conspicuous, so that this appears as the essential message. But where does this balance result from? Why is there such a balance? Let us look again at the pans, isn't the heart[154] firstly and very practically speaking the organ of the circulation? We know how fond the ancient Egyptians were of the concrete[155] and of its representation.[156] As for the feather, it recalls birds, which can fly from Earth to skies and *vice versa*, like the light or solar energy.[157] Through its lightness the feather symbolizes an immaterial energy, through its white color it recalls the white color of the sun light.[158] The feather recalling the bird, free animal traveling from Earth to skies and *vice versa*, is a symbolic representation of the cosmic energy or solar energy, which like birds is free to circulate. As the feather of Maat is in one pan and the heart in the other scale pan, a link is suggested between these two elements. Many Egyptian texts explain indeed that the heart is the organ which receives Maat and also emits Maat. This role of reception-emission of Maat played by the heart is the way by which men participate in maintaining the balance of the cosmic as well as the human world and the free flow of life. The way the heart is pictured, i.e. as a vase, also suggests that the heart can receive Maat and that we can pour Maat out of it. Hence the SCENE, observed without preconceived ideas, portrays the cosmic circulation of life very simply and globally. But a materialistic as well as texts-influenced approach to this picture prevented the scholars from accessing this global knowledge. They forgot that the primary aim of the use of scales is exchange, and there cosmic exchange of Maat.[159] In other words the picture shows the balance obtained through the right circulation of

Maat through the heart. The ancient Egyptians seemed to have some precise and now lost knowledge about the circulation of solar energy. They applied it to many aspects of life and within them to justice, through the concept of Maat. The ancient Egyptians paid attention to life energy and to the fact that any living being on Earth, and even the smallest worm, as they said, participates in the flow of the cosmic energy. The essential message we draw from the picture is the role played by the heart in the flow of Maat. Such a role is undoubtedly confirmed by the Egyptian entire literature, in the texts of philosophy, the texts of wisdom and even in some passages of the *Book Of The Dead*. Within this literature it is easy to find information related to the functioning of the heart with regard to Maat.

In summary, the careful observation of the picture allows us to assert the following points:

1°) The main symbolism of the SCENE does not reveal ethical considerations,[160] only the texts of the confession allow them to appear.[161] There is no obligation to link this SCENE with the texts as *the Egyptian Book Of The Dead* is known to be a compilation of very ancient and sometimes unrelated spells.[162]

2°) On the contrary the SCENE depicts a natural automatic physical and cosmic law. Nobody makes a decision, they all watch the result of the scales. If the pans are in balance, this shows that life (Maat) circulates through the heart, and there is no need for a any kind of judgment.

3°) A certain state of the heart allows the flow of Maat. This flow involves a balance opening the way to life (more life). A heart closed to Maat -i.e. that does not receive and hence cannot emit Maat- prevents reaching the balance and opens the way to disharmony -i.e. less life or a second death as the ancient Egyptians said-. The animal portrayed in the scene and perceived by scholars as a frightening monster is only the way the ancient Egyptians portrayed the principle of death. Look well at "Ammit", "The Great Devourer!" The ancient Egyptians did not place a "monster" in this SCENE for fun.

We know that the artists were not allowed to draw what they pleased, instead they had to follow strict rules imposed by the priests. Ammit shows symbolically how death occurs.

This animal is not made up by parts from different animals for artistic purposes. Since it has a big open mouth and looks disharmonious, Ammit symbolically represents that death occurs because when there is no Maat (life energy) disharmony occurs, which leads to the decomposition of the body and its disappearance. The big open mouth symbolizes disintegration, annihilation and ultimate disappearance. So ”the great devourer“ is not a ”monster“ as the rational mind may perceive it. It is the symbolic way the ancient Egyptians used to explain that death "eats" Man through using the principle of decomposition, when Man has obstructed the flow of life in the body.

4°) The characters are waiting only for the results of the scales, which does not symbolize in this context a concrete weighing but the capability of the heart for exchange. Being the symbol of exchange, the pair of scales also leads to the idea of circulation.

5°) Further information can probably be found in this very global picture and could also be researched in the whole Egyptian imagery. Scholars should make more use of pictures when translating ancient texts, which are often hard for modern minds to understand. Paying more attention to pictures could avoid waste of time and mistranslations.

Finally, we should remember the following ideas:

- Law of balance: a balance of the scales allows the flow of the immaterial solar energy and the expansion of life (to which are related, according to the ancient Egyptians: happiness, good health, freedom and prosperity).[163]
- Only a free flow of energy (flow of Maat through the heart) allows us to reach this balance.

Now in order to confirm the understanding of the SCENE we are going to examine what Maat really was to the ancient Egyptians, and how they considered the heart. We have already seen through the careful observation of the SCENE that Maat is a cosmic energy: solar energy. Now, let us see how scholars view Maat.

CHAPTER 4

JUSTICE AS A KEY TO UNVEIL ANCIENT EGYPT

Jan ASSMANN[164] believes that if we were able to understand the meaning of Maat, we would get a key to understanding the ancient Egyptian world. But this concept is extremely difficult for our modern minds to understand, for the two following reasons:

1°) Eric HORNUNG underlined that in modern languages no word related to law matches Maat,[165] however we ever try to compare Maat, the goddess of justice, with concepts we are used to dealing with in the legal modern world. Scholars reckon that the ancient Egyptians did not pass on to us a clear definition of what Maat is. In fact the Egyptians gave many "Egyptian definitions" of Maat, especially in the rituals of the offering of Maat. The truth is that, whenever we try to find in Maat a concept of justice, in accordance with our modern values, we cannot understand the very clear definitions the Egyptians gave of Maat.

2°) A second main reason is that modern world has the intellectual habit of dealing with great problems by dividing them in smaller questions and in many fields of expertise. This behavior is totally opposite to the Egyptian mind where all the aspects of life and knowledge were integrated.[166] Hence, how can it be possible to have a sound understanding of the concept of Maat if we artificially isolate it, especially from its partner on the scales: the heart? Regarding the heart there is much valuable information we can collect from the Egyptian literature. The information useful to the understanding of Maat is mainly related to the functioning of the human body and heart. As already shown, Egyptian literature is very heterogeneous,[167] hence we must select the valuable information it contains. Almost the whole of Egyptian literature contains information of unequal wisdom and value, and from diverse periods. All this information is often intermingled in the same text, sometime even in the same sentence.[168] Jean YOYOTTE emphasized that the "judgment of the dead" is made of information from different schools of thought. Indeed the ancient Egyptians -like the soil of Egypt[169]- do not easily discard the past, they simply add to it. This explains why we can find in a same text various strata of thinking and many contradictions.[170] The scribes often assert that they get information from very ancient sources.[171] This is particularly true for the *Book Of The Dead*, inspired by former texts, notably, the Pyramids Texts.[172] Along the course of history this book has received additions and has come to reflect the increasing fear of the Egyptian people regarding the afterlife.[173] Hence we cannot use Egyptian literature in the way we would use modern texts. Nor can we evaluate it the same way. I.e. we cannot consider a text to be a totally useless source when, for example it is mainly composed of magic. Even in this case useful information can be mixed with magic. Therefore when dealing with Egyptian literature, we must be more tolerant, and above all able to select valuable information without *a priori*.

In order to unveil the Egyptian concept of Maat, we are going to select from Egyptian literature the permanent information related to Maat, the sun, the functioning of the human body, and especially to the heart. Pierre GRIMAL has already advised, that when speaking about the Egyptian taste for repetition we need to change our attitude.[174] This advice is very valuable and we shall follow it in order to try to understand the concept of Maat better and to be able to reconstitute a coherent picture of the Egyptian concept of justice. To do so, we have searched through Egyptian literature for useful information for the comprehension of Maat. While a large amount of information on Maat is available, a coherent definition of Maat has never been drawn from it. The main reason, as we already mentioned, is that Maat has been studied apart from elements that were necessary to its sound understanding. Another reason is our weakness for imposing modern concepts onto Egyptian concepts. Along with the presentation of the valuable information we have selected, we shall give the Egyptian sources in the footnotes. The collected information will allow us to answer the following points:

- definition of Maat and of its opposite,
- how the flow of Maat produces positive results,
- how Maat circulates in human society,
- what obstructs the right flow of Maat in human society,

- how Maat allows us to understand the unity of all the spheres of life in Egypt,
- why Maat is not actually justice, though she is, as well as the heart, one of its essential components.

1. What is Maat, and what is its opposite?

Through the texts we know that Maat is a cosmic energy which reaches human beings through the sun,[175] through the gods and also through the Pharaoh. We can even find the definition of Maat in one of Rameses II's names: Usermaatra-Setepenra which means: "Maat is the strength of Ra, the beloved of Ra".[176] This cosmic energy manifested as light[177] or power[178] on the human level is also manifested as happiness, good health, strength, life,[179] prosperity, stability (i.e. horizontality, righteousness,[180] balance) and harmony. A passage from the *Coffin Texts* clearly states that Maat is life.[181] We can also understand Maat through the opposite results of the absence of Maat.[182] Without Maat, there is darkness, no harmony, loss of life force, poverty, illness, destruction, death. In the Egyptian language the opposite of Maat is "Isfet".[183] Like the concept of Maat, it is hardly understandable and the many different translations proposed are considered to be approximate by the experts. One among them considers it to be a very unclear word,[184] while Jean YOYOTTE considers that this word can be translated into "chaos".[185] We know through many texts that Maat destroys the enemies of Ra[186] and that darkness is the major enemy of Ra.[187] Hence if Maat is the light creating life, it is easy to see in Isfet, the darkness involving death. This way we can better understand why in the hieroglyphic writing the drawing of a solar black disk means the non-being[188] and also why Maat should not be offered to the god of war.[189] A passage from a *Hymn To Khnum* considers light to be life.[190] This view of Maat also clarifies the following passage of Ani's *Book Of The Dead*: "Chapter LXXX Spell to make the transformation into god who gives the light in the darkness", where Maat is in Ani's body and where Ani says he is the woman who enlightens the darkness.[191] On a cosmic level, the flow of Maat involves the cosmic balance, where the "stability" of Ra (the sun) in the sky is essential to the ancient Egyptians. Maat is the energy that feeds the whole cosmos. Maat feeds the sun, which also breathes her,[192] she feeds all the gods. This makes more clear one of the hieroglyphic writing of Maat, the plinth  recalling the basis of things and also horizontality.

2. The law of Maat and its positive results

In order to produce good results, Maat must flow without obstructions. From there comes the importance, often emphasized by the experts, of the ritual of the offering of Maat to the sun. With this ritual the Pharaoh maintained the cosmic flow by returning to the sun the Maat he (the sun) received through the heart and generously retransmitted. It is through this ritual that the Pharaoh partakes in the cosmic order, while any human being can do the same with a physical organ: the heart. As for the sun, it makes all the hearts[193] live, it breathes Maat,[194] its energy enters in the hearts[195] while the heart is the root of life of every human being.[196] The heart is omnipresent in the Egyptian literature and many expressions are created from it. The ancient Egyptian listens with the heart,[197] understands with the heart, speaks with the heart, makes a decision with the heart,[198] wants with the heart,[199] is guided in his life by the heart.[200]. He lives thanks to the heart,[201] speaks of the heart of the sun and the gods, unites himself to the sun through the heart, unites himself with the heart of his ba,[202] has a righteous heart,[203] is under the protection of the heart while sleeping,[204] lives during the day thanks to the energy of the heart. When the heart is tired his members are weak. Sometimes the animal's heart cries.[205] In short, information on the heart is very rich[206] and makes it easy to understand how Maat circulates in human society.

3. The flow of Maat among people

Maat flows in society through the hearts of men, hence the importance of taking note of the passages in Egyptian literature containing permanent information related to the heart. Hence also the necessity not to distort them. The literal translation often mentioned by experts appears to have much more practical meaning that the non literal translations. The non literal translations the authors made are too often marked by our modern minds and its abstract approach to religion and by our materialistic approach to the world. The literal translation put in the context of the Egyptian specific mentality and sensitivity has a more accurate as well as a more useful meaning. To the Egyptian mind, the heart is the life-giving center -i.e. very practically speaking the one which feeds and transmits life, like a mother-. But let us come back to Maat. The texts tell that the circulation of Maat is more or less good. In the SCENE, we noticed that the heart was pictured as a vase and we deduced from this fact the container role played by the human heart. In fact we know through many texts that the heart receives Maat from the sun,[207] it picks it up through the hearing[208] and through the senses. In the chapter XVIII of Ani's papyrus we can read that Ani has a heart full of Maat.[209] We know by the Prophecies of Neferti that when solar disk is veiled, men are deaf.[210]

The heart is the physical means of the circulation of energy.[211] The benefit which can be drawn from the law of the flowing or non-flowing of an intangible energy through a tangible body or device which "conveys the power"[212] seems to have been understood by the ancient Egyptians before the age of information technology.[213] The SCENE is a remarkable global way to express this knowledge. If the heart is open to Maat, i.e. if it receives well, if it "hears the cosmic energy well",[214] this is a good thing, but it is not enough to create harmony. The energy must circulate too, i.e. it must be correctly emitted and mainly through the tongue (this means through speech) and through actions (that is to say the behavior as well as the gesture). Hence we can understand why speech was so essential to the ancient Egyptians and also why so many civilizations have from a legal point of view given so great an importance to the "promise", or to the strict observance of the "spells of the law" in the ancient Roman law. The speech is Maat. It is Maat received in the heart,[215] transformed and emitted from the tongue. Hence the speech is solar energy flowing into humanity as a whole.

4. The obstacles to the free flow of Maat

The circulation of Maat can be obstructed in many ways. Among these we find especially lies,[216] abhorred by the gods according to the ancient Egyptians. But the word "lie" in Egypt, as we know thanks to many texts, has a very specific and concrete meaning. Above all, it does not refer to any kind of morals. In the Egyptian world, to lie consists in not speaking (and also probably not acting) according to what is felt in the heart, in other words not in compliance with Maat. A liar disturbs the flow of Maat which results in imbalance in himself and around him. The lie is indeed the abhorrence of the gods, as it hinders the correct flow of Maat. The very first victim of the lie is the liar himself. In this very life he will suffer from physical as well as psychical disorders involved by the incorrect flow of energy in him. On the other hand, truth is loved by the ancient Egyptians and has also a very specific and non-moral meaning. To tell the truth means to be fair. One tells the truth when he speaks according to the heart, that is to say according to the correct flow of Maat.[217] Hence speaking the truth means living in compliance with Maat, with the appropriate circulation of energy through the cosmos and through the human society considered as forming part of the cosmos. It is therefore easier to understand the Egyptian expression "fair of voice".[218] It just means that the voice is fair when it is emitted in compliance with the heart, that is to say in compliance with the right flow of Maat. As the *Text Of Memphite Theology*[219] explains, one of the results of such a fair voice is creativity, inventiveness due to the emission of life energy through the voice. Another way to hinder the flow of Maat is "the greed of the heart" the Egyptian condemned[220] so vividly. Nevertheless the greed of the heart, as well as lie or truth, does not involve ethical and moral values. It is not a sin as the modern mind would believe it. To the Egyptians the greed of the heart is only a malfunction[221] of the heart, which can be corrected. A man with a greedy heart is unable to exchange, and to make Maat circulate. He is the first who suffers from this malfunction of the heart; as he does not receive all the good things Maat conveys.[222]

A third way of obstructing the flow of Maat consists in "swallowing the heart" or "eating the heart".[223] We could not find the clear meaning of these expressions within Egyptian literature. They seem to refer to a lack of exchange, something like a "close circuit".

A fourth manner of obstructing the flow of Maat consists in inability to receive it. This occurs mainly when the "hearing" is bad. While the lightness of the heart is a good quality to the modern world, it is a defect to the ancient Egyptian world. To them lightness of the heart was not an abstract and moral concept. Hence having a light heart was far from being a good thing. It meant not having enough Maat in the heart, and in consequence being not sufficiently alive.[224] A text states that the lightness of the heart results in heaviness in bodily gesture.[225] While *a contrario* another text mentions that being full of Maat brings corporal good health.[226] As we know that lightness of the heart was a defect and not a quality to the ancient Egyptians, we have one more reason to refuse the scholars' view of the SCENE. Their approach to the heart is a clear illustration of the way we impose our modern ideas onto ancient Egypt. Our morals and the idea of sin, which was unknown to the ancient Egyptians, hinder us from understanding them.

5. Maat: the link between all the spheres of life

Maat is omnipresent, she animates all that has a heart and,

according to the *Text Of Memphite Theology,* any living thing has a heart. The Egyptian texts often state that Maat is the daughter of the sun, but also his mother, his food and also the food of all the gods. As a mother and a daughter of Ra, the feminine aspect of the symbol is emphasized. Through this feminine symbol the ancient Egyptians pictured the law of the circulation of life (or cosmic energy or solar energy). What truly characterizes the feminine body is its ability to transmit life and to feed it. A woman, like the sun, lets the (immaterial) life pass through her (physical) body. The correct circulation of Maat in the universe results in what the Egyptians called "stability", "horizontality" or "righteousness", as many words for our modern concept of balance.[227] The "stability" also refers to the essential result of the correct circulation of solar energy: cosmic harmony. In the Egyptian context, being "righteous" or "fair" means acting in conformity with Maat. That is to say letting Maat circulate, in other words causing no obstruction to the circulation of Maat. Very pragmatically, the Egyptian words "right"[228] and "horizontal" referred to the position of the scale pans.[229] All the human beings are linked together by the circulation of Maat through their hearts. Even the sun has a heart.[230] In consequence, Maat appears naturally to be the reason why, in ancient Egypt, all the aspects of life -social, political, scientific as well as what we perceive as religious- were united. All was considered under the angle of circulation of Maat as an energy. This energy angle, which was of high interest to the ancient Egyptians, is widely ignored by our modern materialistic approach to the human society. The Egyptians believed that the continuing flow of life-force maintained the cosmic, as well as the political balance. Through the ritual of the offering of Maat, the Pharaoh ended the circle of energy exchange. He received indeed Maat from the sun and he returned Maat to the sun. In this way, he participated in the cosmic circulation of Maat and in the balance of the universe. Hence we understand why the ritual of the offering of Maat was the main ritual. In fact, what we called "Egyptian religion" had nothing to do with our modern and abstract notion of religion.[231] The results of the right circulation of Maat or the results of its wrong circulation were not abstractions but could be experienced by anyone.

Anyone could for example notice the effect of the bad circulation of Maat in the body and could correct the wrong behavior consequently.[232] The ancient Egyptians indeed did not speak of sins but of malfunction that should be corrected by adopting a behavior in compliance with Maat, by a better "hearing" of Maat.[233]

The ancient Egyptian world was focused on two main aims depending on the correct circulation of Maat. One was inner well-being: good health, happiness, vitality; the other was external material prosperity.[234] This material prosperity was also closely dependent on the right circulation of Maat.[235] Light and white,[236] Maat is an energy (solar energy, cosmic energy or life force) which must circulate. The Egyptian people were mainly seeking happiness and vitality and the repeated wish addressed to the Pharaoh was: "life -good health- strength". As Claire LALOUETTE explains, this was the abbreviation for the sentence: "May he live, be in good health and prosperous".[237] This sentence was placed after the writing of each royal name, or after the writing of each element of the person of the king or after the writing of the names of people close to him.[238] As the modern world lacks interest in the inner prosperity of human beings, we know very little about human energy. Though we know that plants receive, transform and emit solar energy, we do not care about the circulation of solar energy through human society. The ancient Egyptians applied their knowledge regarding the flow of solar energy in order to create physical wealth successfully. Now, let us define what justice was to the Ancient Egyptians.

6. Maat is not the actual Egyptian justice

Though Maat, as well as the heart, is the main component of justice, Maat is not in herself justice. Maat is so necessary to the concept of justice that it is not surprising that generations of Egyptologists and Historians of religions wrongly believed Maat to be the Egyptian justice. They translated Maat into the expression "Goddess of Truth-Justice", Justice, Truth or even order. Though they were embarrassed by the vagueness of this translation they were aware of the difficulty for modern minds in understanding so specific an ancient Egyptian concept. To do Maat means to do energy, to say Maat means to "say energy" or in modern words to make energy circulates. To do Maat, to be fair, to be balanced, to be right, to be horizontal, to be stable all consists in letting Maat circulate correctly, through a correct use of the heart and also of the tongue.

7. What is the ancient Egyptian justice?

White and light Maat is not justice, but justice consists in letting Maat flow correctly. To dispense justice is therefore to re-establish the correct circulation of Maat or to impede obstruction to the correct flow of Maat. As it pictures the idea of justice in ancient Egypt, the SCENE should be more appropriately called "the scene of justice". Finally, the ancient Egyptian concept of justice appears to be very different from our abstract and modern idea of justice. In Egypt, justice was a life process consisting in establishing or re-establishing, through the balance between matter and energy, the correct and harmonious flow of cosmic energy (of which speech is one of the external human manifestations). Such a concept of justice is valid on a cosmic level, as well as on a human level. To render justice is to have the scale pans at the same level, "right" or "stable". In order to achieve this result, the Egyptians had to hear Maat,[239] to say Maat, to do Maat. That is to say to receive Maat well and to emit Maat well. The ancient Egyptians also spoke of the stability of the sun, and stability was one of the good wishes addressed to the Pharaoh.[240]

CONCLUSION

Through the study of the ancient Egyptian concept of Maat, we have found an idea of justice which is very different from the one effective in our modern world. In the modern world, justice mainly consists of sharing[241] material goods, amounts of money and honors, and punishing people, whereas the aim of Egyptian justice was quite different. The Egyptian concept of justice is very original and its aim is to increase life and to allow physical wealth as well as personal intangible prosperity and happiness. In the Egyptian world, each human being is part of the cosmos. As "living matter" he has the ability to receive solar energy through the heart, to transform it and to send it back out. One of the famous ways he emits solar energy is through speech: the *logos*. The ancient Egyptians had believed that a harmonious flow of solar energy, when transformed into words, involved growth on many levels: inner-growth, inner-happiness, outer growth through physical and material prosperity. They also believed that the obstruction of the flow of energy would mean a crisis: destruction, misery and even death. Even if archeological remains prove that Egyptians applied this knowledge to the sphere of solar energy, they did not just limit themselves to that field. The ancient Egyptians, like other ancient peoples, understood the importance of the proper flow of thought. They had also understood how much physical as well as intangible exchanges bring wealth in the tangible as well as in the intangible world. The fact that Maat is the central concept of Egyptian civilization would imply that the ancient Egyptian priests had a sound knowledge of the properties of solar energy and of the processes of life and death.

NOTES

[1]. While in Babylon the Hammurabi Code received from the sun-god, *cf.* SARRAF Joseph, *op. cit.*, p.31.

[2]. *Cf.* LALOUETTE Claire, *Textes sacrés et Textes profanes de l'Ancienne Egypte, volume II: Mythes, contes et poésies*, Paris, Gallimard/Unesco, 1987, p. 84: about the first International treaty, dated of the year 1278 B.C, Between RAMESES II ET HATTUSILI III.

[3]. *Ibid*, SARRAF Joseph, introduction.

[4]. From the present knowledge in Egyptology, we know that the weighing of the souls has become individual around 2000 B.C. Before that time it was reserved to the King.

[5]. The spelling of Maat by the authors varies.

[6]. For example: SARRAF Joseph, *La notion du droit d'après les Anciens Egyptiens*, Città del Vaticano, *op. cit.*, p. 35; Jan ASSMANN, *Maât, l'Egypte pharaonique et l'idée de justice sociale*, Conférences essais et leçons du Collège de France, Paris, Julliard, 1989, p. 104; MORET Alexandre, *Le Nil et la civilisation égyptienne*, Paris, La Renaissance du livre, 1926, p. 440.

[7]. *Cf.* for example: YOYOTTE Jean, "La pensée préphilosophique en Egypte", Paris excerpt from the Encyclopédie de la Pléiade, histoire de la philosophie, I, 19., p. 11.

[8]. GOYON Jean-Claude, *Maât et Pharaon ou de destin de l'Egypte antique*, Lyon, Editions ACV, 1998, p. 88.

[9]. TEETER Emily, *The Presentation Of Maat, Ritual And Legitimacy In Ancient Egypt,* Chicago, The University of Chicago, 1997.

[10]. TEETER Emily, *op. cit.* p. 14-15.

[11]. Here are some symbolic representions of the goddess Maat:

 the white feather.  the base  the goddess.

[12]. GOYON Jean-Claude, *op. cit.*, p. 88.

[13]. LICHTHEIM Myriam, *Maat In Egyptian Autobiographies And Related Studies*, Universitätsverlag Freiburg Schweiz, Vandenthoeck and Ruprecht Göttingen, 1992.

[14]. But not the lawyers.

[15]. FRANKFORT Henri, *Ancient Egyptian Religion, An Interpretation*, New York, Columbia University Press, 1948, passim.

[16]. ASSMANN Jan, *op. cit.* p. 18; FRANKFORT Henri, *Ancient Egyptian Religion, op. cit.* p. 67, p. 117-118.

[17]. ASSMANN Jan, *op. cit.* p. 144, note 11; DERCHAIN Philippe, *Le papyrus Salt 825 (BM 10051) rituel pour la conservation de la vie en Egypte*, Bruxelles, Académie royale de Belgique, Mémoire n° 1784, Classe des lettres, volume LVIII, fasc. I a, 1965, p. 13.

[18]. BLEEKER Claas Jouco, De beteekenis van de egyptische godin Ma-a-t, Leiden, 1929.

[19]. BLEEKER Claas Jouco, *Egyptians Festivals, Enactments Of Religious Renewal*, Leiden, Netherlands, E.J. Brill, 1967,

[20]. BLEEKER Claas Jouco, *Egyptians Festivals, op. cit.*, p 1

[21]. BLEEKER Claas Jouco, *Egyptians Festivals, op. cit.*, p. 4.

[22]. BLEEKER Claas Jouco, *Egyptians Festivals, op. cit.*, p. 16.

[23]. BLEEKER Claas Jouco, *Egyptians Festivals, op. cit.*, p. 12-13.

[24]. BLEEKER Claas Jouco, *Egyptians Festivals, op. cit.*, p.7-8.

[25]. BLEEKER Claas Jouco, *Egyptians Festivals, op. cit.*, p.6-7.

[26]. BLEEKER Claas Jouco, *Egyptians Festivals, op. cit.*, p. 7.

[27]. BLEEKER Claas Jouco, *De Beteekenis Van De Egyptische Godin Ma-a-t, Leiden*, 1929.

[28]. SHIRUN-GRUMACH Irene, "Remarks On The Goddess MAAT", *Pharaonic Egypt, The Bible And Christianity*, Jerusalem, edition S. Israelit-Groll, the Magnes Press, The Hebrew University, 1985, 173-201.: *cf* p. 173: "I am deeply indebted to Bleeker in whose book on Maat a rather similar concept is presented: the feather of Shu and

Maat suggests a "cosmogonic" relationship between the two in the light of their part in creation: Shu divides heaven and earth and Maat is the power nourishing and renewing the sun-god. Their feather is understood as the symbol of not only air but also light in view of this. Maat is not seen as a "personal goddess" though, as Bleeker's study in its general outline presents her as (cosmic and ethic) "order" personified, an approach which has become the foundation for current research."

[29]. BLEEKER Claas Jouco, *Egyptians Festivals, op. cit.*, p. 5, he quotes MORENZ who underlined the fact that the Egyptian language does not contain some words: MORENZ, *Ägyptische Religion*, 1960 "He is the first to have pointed out that the Egyptian language has no words for concepts such as religion, piety and belief, which are an integral part of our language... But the picture he presents of ancient Egyptian religion as such, is too much centred on individual piety and gives a biased and distorted view of important facets of the object of study, viz. the cult."

[30]. DERCHAIN Philippe, *Le papyrus Salt 825 (BM 10051) rituel pour la conservation de la vie en Egypte*, Bruxelles, Académie royale de Belgique, Mémoire n° 1784, Classe des lettres, volume LVIII, fasc. I a, 1965, p. 13.

[31]. HORNUNG Erik, *L'esprit du temps des pharaons*, Paris, Hachette, collection Pluriel, 1996, p. 137.

[32]. BLEEKER Claas Jouco, *Egyptians Festivals, op. cit.*, p. 6.

[33]. BLEEKER Claas Jouco, *Egyptians Festivals, op. cit.*, p. 6

[34]. Myth creation.

[35]. FRANKFORT H, FRANKFORT A, WILSON, JACOBSON AND IRWIN, *The Intellectual Adventure Of Ancient Man*, Chicago, University of Chicago Press, 1946, p. 10.

[36]. FRANKFORT Henri, *Ancient Egyptian Religion, An Interpretation*, New York, Columbia University Press, 1948.

[37]. FRANKFORT Henri, *Ancient Egyptian Religion, An Interpretation*, New York, Columbia University Press, 1948, p. 63.

[38]. FRANKFORT Henri, *Ancient Egyptian Religion, An Interpretation,* New York, Columbia University Press, 1948 p. 93, 108, 109, 114.

[39]. FRANKFORT Henri, *Ancient Egyptian Religion, An Interpretation*, *op. cit.*, p.19.

[40]. FRANKFORT Henri, *Ancient Egyptian Religion, An Interpretation*, *op. cit.*, p. 90.

[41]. FRANKFORT Henri, *Ancient Egyptian Religion, An Interpretation*, *op. cit.*, p. 55.

[42]; FRANKFORT Henri, *Ancient Egyptian Religion, An Interpretation*, New York, Columbia University Press, 1948 p. 51, *cf.* also on this theme: Henri FRANKFORT, *Kingship And The Gods*, Chicago, 1948.

[43]. FRANKFORT Henri, *Ancient Egyptian Religion, An Interpretation*, *op. cit*., p. 55.

[44]. FRANKFORT Henri, *Ibid,* p. 117.

[45]. FRANKFORT Henri, *Ibid,* p. 73.

[46]. On this concept, *cf.* TZITZIS Stamatios, *Esthétique de la Violence*, Paris, PUF, 1997, p. 6.

[47]. FRANKFORT Henri, *ibid,* p. 73.

[48]. FRANKFORT Henri, *ibid,* p. 117.

[49]. FRANKFORT Henri, *ibid,* p. 117-118.

[50]. FRANKFORT Henri, *ibid,* p. 118-119.

[51]. FRANKFORT Henri, *ibid,* p. 121.

[52]. FRANKFORT Henri, *ibid,* p. 72, on the practical effect of being generous.

[53]. ASSMANN Jan, *Maât, l'Egypte pharaonique et l'idée de justice sociale*, Conférences essais et leçons du Collège de France, Paris, Julliard, 1989.

[54]. ASSMANN Jan, *Maât, l'Egypte pharaonique et l'idée de justice sociale*, *op. cit*., p. 12.

[55]. ASSMANN Jan, *Maât, l'Egypte pharaonique et l'idée de justice sociale*, *op. cit*., p. 13.

[56]. ASSMANN Jan, *Maât, l'Egypte pharaonique et l'idée de justice sociale*, *op. cit*., p. 17.

[57]. ASSMANN Jan, *Maât, l'Egypte pharaonique et l'idée de justice sociale*, *op. cit*., p. 18.

[58]. ASSMANN Jan, *Maât, l'Egypte pharaonique et l'idée de justice sociale*, *op. cit*., p. 18.

[59]. ASSMANN Jan, *Maât, l'Egypte pharaonique et l'idée de justice sociale*, *op. cit.*, *cf* pp. 54-55.

[60]. In French: "L'homme de l'oasis".

[61]. ASSMANN Jan, *Maât, l'Egypte pharaonique et l'idée de justice sociale*, *op. cit.*, p. 36.

[62]. That is to say (in this patriarchal society where the instructions of wisdom collected are always dedicated to sons) to listen and to obey the father.

[63]. *Cf.* "La prophétie de Neferty", translated by Claire LALOUETTE, *Textes sacrés et Textes profanes de l'Ancienne Egypte*, volume I: *Des Pharaons et des Hommes*, 1984, Gallimard/Unesco, p. 71.

[64]. TOMATIS Alfred, *Vers l'écoute humaine*, Paris, E.S.F., 1979, volume 1, p. 34, translated from French: "L'oreille, en effet, n'a pas été conçue pour entendre. Comment dès lors le serait-elle pour écouter? Elle doit assurer deux fonctions majeures qui répondent, en réalité, à une seule et même activité: l'équilibre et la recharge du système nerveux en énergie. Ce n'est que secondairement qu'elle va se mettre à entendre et, plus tard, à écouter".

[65]. COPPENS Yves, *Le Genou de Lucy*, Paris, Poches Odile Jacob, 2000, p. 27.

[66]. ASSMANN Jan, *Maât, l'Egypte pharaonique et l'idée de justice sociale*, *op. cit.*, p. 107.

[67]. ASSMANN Jan, *Maât, l'Egypte pharaonique et l'idée de justice sociale*, *op. cit.*, p. 37, translated from French: "Agis pour celui qui agit."

[68]. ASSMANN Jan, *Maât, l'Egypte pharaonique et l'idée de justice sociale*, *op. cit.*, p. 133.

[69]. BICKEL S., *La cosmogonie égyptienne avant le Nouvel Empire*, Fribourg, 1999, p. 171.

[70]. MENU Bernadette, "Le tombeau de Pétosiris (2) Maât, Thot et le droit", Paris, *BIFAO* (*Bulletin de l'Institut Français d'Archéologie Orientale*), volume 95 (1995), p. 281-295.

[71]. MENU Bernadette, *ibid.*, p. 282.

[72]. According to Pierre GRIMAL, in the preface to: LALOUETTE Claire, *Textes sacrés et Textes profanes de l'Ancienne Egypte*, volume I, *Des Pharaons et des Hommes*, Paris, Gallimard/Unesco, 1984, p. 8 and p. 16.

[73]. According to Karl JASPERS, cf. previous note n°9.

[74]. In English: "The pre-philosophical thought in Egypt", YOYOTTE Jean, "La pensée préphilosophique en Egypte", Paris 19.., pp. 1-23. extr. Encyclopédie de la Pléiade, histoire de la philosophie, I.

[75]. YOYOTTE Jean,"La pensée préphilosophique en Egypte", *op. cit.,* p. 1. This opinion is also shared by all the authors whether they are Egyptologists or Historians of religions, *cf.* for example:FRANKFORT H., FRANKFORT A., WILSON, JACOBSON AND IRWIN, *The Intellectual Adventure Of Ancient Man*, 1946, University of Chicago Press, p. 3; BLEEKER Claas Jouco, *Egyptians Festivals, Enactments Of Religious Renewal*, 1967, *op. cit.*, p. 14; Beatrice L. GOFF, *Symbols Of Ancient*

Egypt In The Late Period, TheTwenty-first Dynasty, Yale University, Mouton publishers, 1979, p. 19.

[76]. YOYOTTE Jean, "La pensée préphilosophique en Egypte", *op. cit.*, p. 2.

[77]. HORNUNG Erik, *L'esprit du temps des Pharaons*, Paris, Hachette,1996, p. 25. For some pictorial examples see: 86 and p. 163.

[78]. HORNUNG Erik, *op. cit.*, p. 16-17.

[79]. GOFF Beatrice L., *Symbols Of Ancient Egypt In The Late Period, The Twenty-first Dynasty*, *op. cit.*, p. 158.

[80]. MORET Alexandre, *Le Nil et la civilisation égyptienne*, Paris, La Renaissance du livre, 1926, p. 422.

[81]. MORET Alexandre, *Le Nil et la civilisation égyptienne*, Paris, La Renaissance du livre, 1926, p. 91; MORENZ Siegfried, Egyptian Religion, London, Methuen and Co litd, 1976, p. 153-154; HORNUNG Erik, *L'esprit du temps des Pharaons*, Hachette, 1996, p. 25.

[82]. IVERSEN Erik, *The Myth Of Egypt And Its Hieroglyphs In European Tradition*, Copenhagen, GEC Gad, 1961, p. II.

[83]. IVERSEN Erik, *op. cit.*, p.11.

[84]. GOFF Beatrice L., *Symbols Of Ancient Egypt In The Late Period, The Twenty-first Dynasty*, *op. cit.*, p. 158 "There are many forms of presentational symbolism, among them, music, ritual, poetry, and art. The elements of discursive symbolism, because they provide precise denotation of ideas, are known as signs. The elements of

presentational symbolism furnish an integral presentation of experience that does not lend itself to precise definition. These elements deal with the connotation of ideas, emotions, intuition".

[85]. In the information technology field we would speak of a compressed file we need to expand.

[86]. On silence as a virtue in the Egyptian world *cf.*: ASSMANN Jan, *Maât, l'Egypte pharaonique et l'idée de justice sociale*, Conférences essais et leçons du Collège de France, Paris, Julliard, 1989, p. 44: "La sagesse en égyptien est le silence"; *cf.* FRANKFORT Henri, *Ancient Egyptian Religion, An Interpretation*, New York, Columbia University Press, 1948, p. 66.

[87]. MORENZ Siegfried, *Egyptian Religion*, London, Methuen and Co ltd, 1976, p. 175: "The second point makes us conscious that for all the interest in science, the idiom employed was that of myth, so that physics never became secularized in Egypt..."; Philippe DERCHAIN, *Rituel pour la conservation de la vie en Egypte*, Bruxelles, Académie royale de Belgique, Mémoire n° 1784, Classe des lettres, volume LVIII, fasc. I a, 1965. p. 4, note 3; PIANKOFF Alexandre, *La création du disque solaire*, IFAO, bibli. 2 volumes 19, p. 7.

[88]. ASSMANN Jan, *Maât, l'Egypte pharaonique et l'idée de justice sociale*, *op. cit.*, p. 17.

[89]. MORENZ Siegfried, *Egyptian Religion*, London, Methuen and Co litd, 1976, p. 175 on the interpenetration between science and religion.

[90]. DERCHAIN Philippe, *Le papyrus Salt 825 (BM 10051) rituel pour la conservation de la vie en Egypte*, Bruxelles, Académie royale de Belgique, Mémoire n° 1784, Classe des lettres, volume LVIII, fasc. I a, 1965.

[91]. DERCHAIN Philippe, *Le papyrus Salt* 825 (BM 10051); *op. cit.,* p. 4, note 3: PIANKOFF Alexandre, *la création du disque solaire*, IFAO, bibli. 2 volumes 19, p. 1.

[92]. DERCHAIN Philippe, *Le papyrus Salt 825 (BM 10051)*; *op. cit.,* p. 4, note 3: PIANKOFF Alexandre, *la création du disque solaire*, IFAO, bibli. 2 volumes 19, p. 7.

[93]. DERCHAIN Philippe, *Le papyrus Salt 825 (BM 10051)*; *op. cit.,* p. 4. *Cf.* also p. 6.

[94]. After having explained, like the other scholars, that the Egyptian rituals are processes of energy exchange between gods and the pharaoh or the king. These rituals are intended to maintain the life flow.

[95]. DERCHAIN Philippe, *Le papyrus Salt 825 (BM 10051)*; *op. cit.,* p. 4. *Cf.* also p. 14 he quotes, note 37: in the same line regarding the Egyptian temple, *cf.* SAUNERON,POSERNER, YOYOTTE, dict. Civ. eg., 1961, 282-283.

[96]. GOYON Jean-Claude, *Maât et Pharaon ou de destin de l'Egypte antique*, Lyon, Editions ACV, 1998, p. 89.

[97]. DERCHAIN Philippe, Le papyrus Salt 825 (BM 10051); *op. cit.*, p. 9.

[98]. HUVELIN Paul, *Les tablettes magiques et le droit romain*, Macon, Protat Frères, 1901, p. 13. On the difference between the modern religious behaviour and the practical religious behaviour of the ancient people, *cf.* POTTER T. W., *Roman Britain*, London, Bristish Museum Press, 1997, p. 74-75.

[99]. DERCHAIN Philippe, Le papyrus Salt 825 (BM 10051); *op. cit.*, p. 17.

[100]. GOYON Jean-Claude, *Maât et Pharaon ou de destin de l'Egypte antique*, Lyon, Editions ACV, 1998, p. 92.

[101]. Archeological remains are all from the Ptolemaic period, according to Philippe DERCHAIN.

[102]. DERCHAIN Philippe, *Le papyrus Salt 825 (BM 10051)*; *op. cit.*, p. 19.

[103]. JUNG Karl Gustav, *L'énergétique psychique*, Genève, Georg éditeur S.A., 1987.

[104]. It is interesting to compare with Chinese acupuncture, that helps energy circulate in the human body. Chinese acupuncture considers also the human being in the cosmic dimension, *cf.* Doctor TRAN TIEN CHANH, *L'acupuncture et le Tao*, Meudon, Editions Partage, 1988, p. 94.

[105]. LALOUETTE Claire, *Textes sacrés et Textes profanes de l'Ancienne Egypte*, volume I, *Des Pharaons et des Hommes*, *op. cit.*, p. 270; FAULKNER Raymond, *The*

Ancient Egyptian Book Of The Dead, British Museum Press, London, 1996, p.12; Ian SHAW and Paul NICHOLSON, *British Museum Dictionary of Ancient Egypt*, London, British Museum Press, 1995, p. 55.

[106]. RACHET Guy, *Le livre des morts des anciens Egyptiens*, *op. cit.*, p. 44.

[107]. YOYOTTE Jean, "Le jugement des morts selon l'Egypte ancienne", *op. cit.*, p. 17.

[108]. YOYOTTE Jean, "Le jugement des morts selon l'Egypte ancienne", Paris, Sources Orientales, IV, 1961, p. 44 and following pages.

[109]. YOYOTTE Jean, "Le jugement des morts selon l'Egypte ancienne", *op. cit.*, p 45.

[110]. FRANKFORT Henri, *Ancient Egyptian Religion, An Interpretation, op. cit.*, pp. 112, 116-11.

[111]. FAULKNER Raymond, *The Ancient Egyptian Book Of The Dead*, British Museum Press, London, 1996, p. 55.

[112]. DRIOTON Etienne, "Le jugement des âmes dans l'Egypte ancienne", Revue du Caire, 1949, p. 1-20, p. 19.

[113]. DRIOTON Etienne, "Le jugement des âmes dans l'Egypte ancienne", *op. cit.*, p. 19, p. 9.

[114]. YOYOTTE Jean, "Le jugement des morts selon l'Egypte ancienne", *op. cit.*, p. 44-45.

[115]. YOYOTTE Jean, "Le jugement des morts selon l'Egypte ancienne", *op. cit.*, p. 45.

[116]. HORNUNG Erik, *L'esprit du temps des pharaons*, Paris, Hachette, 1996, p. 9.

[117]. HORNUNG Erik, *L'esprit du temps des pharaons*, *op. cit.*, p.15, p. 16.

[118]. HORNUNG Erik, *L'esprit du temps des pharaons*, *op. cit.*, p.18.

[119]. HORNUNG Erik, *L'esprit du temps des pharaons*, *op. cit.*, p.31.

[120]. HORNUNG Erik, *L'esprit du temps des pharaons*, *op. cit.*, p. 135. However we can agree with his analysis of the hieroglyph used to represent Maat and which is a base. .

[121]. On the Egyptian writing *cf.* HORNUNG ERIK, *op. cit.*, p. 18. Comp. with the ancient Rome where writing was also sacred: HUVELIN Paul, *op. cit.*, p. 11.

[122]. *Cf.* AMELINEAU Emile, *La morale égyptienne quinze siècles avant notre ère, Etude sur le papyrus de Boulaq n° 4*, Paris, Editions Ernest Leroux, 1892, p. XVIII.

[123]. This was also the case of the sculptors, MORET Alexandre, *Le Nil et la civilisation égyptienne*, Paris, La Renaissance du livre, 1926, p. 422 and also 498.

[124]. Emile AMELINEAU underlined with lucidity and realism that texts like the *Book Of The Dead*, he qualified as "book of Horror" (livre des épouvantements) let clearly appear the interests of the priests regarding their "custom".

[125]. ASSMANN Jan, *Maât, l'Egypte pharaonique et l'idée de justice sociale*, *op. cit.*, p. 28.

[126]. YOYOTTE Jean, "Le jugement des morts selon l'Egypte ancienne", *op. cit.*, p. 12.

[127]. MORET Alexandre, "La doctrine de Maât", *op. cit.*, p. 1-14.

[128]. MORET Alexandre, "Le jugement des morts, en Egypte et hors d'Egypte", *op. cit.*, p.257.

[129]. YOYOTTE Jean, "Le jugement des morts selon l'Egypte ancienne", *op. cit.*, p. 46.

[130]. ASSMANN Jan, *Maât, l'Egypte pharaonique et l'idée de justice sociale*, *op. cit.*, 1989

[131]. ASSMANN Jan, *Maât, l'Egypte pharaonique et l'idée de justice sociale*, *op. cit.*, p. 72.

[132]. ASSMANN Jan, *Maât, l'Egypte pharaonique et l'idée de justice sociale*, *op. cit.*, p. 72.

[133]. ASSMANN Jan, *Maât, l'Egypte pharaonique et l'idée de justice sociale*, *op. cit.*, p. 73.

[134]. ASSMANN Jan, *Maât, l'Egypte pharaonique et l'idée de justice sociale*, *op. cit.*, p. 80.

[135]. ASSMANN Jan, *Maât, l'Egypte pharaonique et l'idée de justice sociale*, *op. cit.*, p. 81.

[136]. ASSMANN Jan, *Maât, l'Egypte pharaonique et l'idée de justice sociale*, *op. cit.* p. 82-83.

[137]. FAULKNER R.O., *The Ancient Egyptian Book Of The Dead*, London, British Museum, 1996, p. 34.

[138]. MORENZ Siegfried, *Egyptian Religion*, *op. cit.*

[139]. MORENZ Siegfried, *Egyptian Religion*, *op. cit.*, p. 131.

[140]. MORENZ Siegfried, *Egyptian Religion*, *op. cit.*, 1976, p. 130.

[141]. MORENZ Siegfried, *Egyptian Religion*, *op. cit.*, London, 1976, p. 126-127.

[142]. "L'homme de l'Oasis" (The peasant) translation by Claire LALOUETTE, *Textes sacrés et Textes profanes de l'Ancienne Egypte*, volume I, *op. cit.,* p. 203: "...car tu dois être une balance".

[143]. "L'homme de l'Oasis", translation by Claire LALOUETTE, *Textes sacrés et Textes profanes de l'Ancienne Egypte*, volume I, *Des Pharaons et des Hommes*, Paris, Gallimard/Unesco, 1984, p. 204.

[144]. FRANKFORT Henri, *Ancient Egyptian Religion, An Interpretation*, *op. cit.*, p. 117-121.

[145]. FRANKFORT Henri, *Ancient Egyptian Religion, An Interpretation*, *op. cit.*, 1948, p. 118-119.

[146]. On the role played by colours in Egypt, *cf.* HORNUNG Erik, *op. cit.*, p.15. White is also the colour of the sun light *cf*: LALOUETTE Claire, *Textes sacrés et Textes profanes de l'Ancienne Egypte*, volume II, *op. cit.*, note p. 290.

[147]. The Ankh cross is the symbol of life.  excerpt from WILSON Hilary, *op. cit.*, p. 46.

[148]. This animal is deemed to devour the soul of the deceased, who when found guilty must die a second time.

[149]. In spite of the magic which will be used more and more frequently in order to force the passage.

[150]. It is the falcon headed god: Horus.

[151]. At the top of the scales we can find Thot, Ra, or Maat. On the pan we can find instead of the feather a statuette of Maat holding the Ankh cross. Sometimes the vase is replaced by a human head. As for the 42 judges their were added later: *Cf.* YOYOTTE Jean, "Le jugement des morts selon l'Egypte ancienne", *op. cit.* p. 59; FRANKFORT Henri, *op. cit.*, p. 118.

[152]. RACHET Guy, *Le livre des morts des anciens Egyptiens*, *op. cit.*, p. 27.

[153]. Erik HORNUNG believes that the balance between the heart and the feather was a magical representation, while to Jan ASSMANN this forms part of an initiation.

[154]. On which modern authors could not prevent to tack our modern concepts of religion, morals, conscience, and ethic.

[155]. On the realism of the Egyptian language, *cf.* Pierre GRIMAL, preface to: LALOUETTE Claire, *Textes sacrés et Textes profanes de l'Ancienne Egypte*, volume I, *Des Pharaons et des Hommes*, op. *cit.*, p. 15, MENU Bernadette. LALOUETTE Claire, *op. cit., volume* 1 p 206, "L'homme de l'Oasis".

[156]. Alexandre MORET quoted a hieroglyphic text stating that "Thot is the fertilizer of Maat", this is rendered by the following very realistic and evocative hieroglyphs where we can see a phallus out of which the sperm is flowing. MORET Alexandre, *Le rituel du culte divin journalier en Egypte*, Paris, Ernest Leroux, 1902, p. 139.

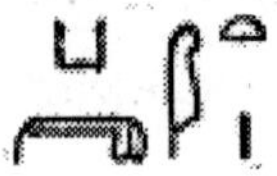

"Ailleurs, Thot est appelé le 'fécondateur de Mâït" (Todtenbuch, CXLI, 14).

[157]. It is also the opinion of SHIRUN-GRUMACH Irene, "Remarks On The Goddess MAAT", *Pharaonic Egypt, the bible and christianity*, *op. cit.*, p. 173.

[158]. *Cf.* LALOUETTE Claire, *Textes sacrés et Textes profanes de l'Ancienne Egypte, volume II: Mythes, contes et poésies*, 1987, Gallimard/Unesco, note p. 290, and p. 161.

[159]. On the symbolism of the scales: *cf.* Jean CHEVALIER, Alain GHEERBRANT, Dictionnaire des symboles, Paris, Laffont, Collection Bouquins, 1982, p. 98.

[160]. FRANKFORT Henri, *Ancient Egyptian Religion, An Interpretation, op. cit.*, p. 118-119.

[161]. The Egyptian texts often appears obscure to our modern minds.

[162]. FAULKNER Raymond, *The Ancient Egyptian Book Of The Dead*, British Museum Press, London, 1996, p. 11, introduction by Carol A. R. ANDREW: "Some of the spells in the *Book Of The Dead* originated in the *Pyramid Texts* which first appeared carved in hieroglyphs on the walls of the burial chamber and anteroom of the pyramid of King Wenis, last ruler of the Fifth Dynasty, about 2345 BC. Although this is their first written appearance this is clear from their content that many of these utterances had been in existence for centuries".

[163]. *Cf.* LALOUETTE Claire, *Textes sacrés et Textes profanes de l'Ancienne Egypte*, volume I: *Des Pharaons et des Hommes*, 1984, *op. cit.*, note 10.

[164]. ASSMANN Jan, *Maât, l'Egypte pharaonique et l'idée de justice sociale*, *op. cit.*, p.13.

[165]. HORNUNG Erik, *L'esprit du temps des pharaons*, Hachette, *op. cit.*, p. 137.

[166]. That is to say the social, the religious, the cosmic, etc.

[167]. RACHET Guy, *Le livre des morts des anciens Égyptiens*, *op. cit.*, p. 48 on Ani's papyrus.

[168]. RACHET Guy, *Le livre des morts des anciens Égyptiens*, *op. cit.*, p. 153. *Cf.* also on this feature of the Egyptian literature: YOYOTTE Jean, "La pensée préphilosophique en Egypte", *op. cit.*, p. 3-4, p. 14, p. 15.

[169]. MORET Alexandre, *Le Nil et la civilisation égyptienne*, *op. cit.*, p. 84-85. *Cf.* on the "Pyramids texts": LALOUETTE Claire, *Textes sacrés et Textes profanes de l'Ancienne Egypte*, volume I: *Des Pharaons et des Hommes*, *op. cit.*, p. 142. *Cf.* GRIMAL Pierre, preface to Claire LALOUETTE, *Textes sacrés et Textes profanes de l'Ancienne Egypte, volume II: Mythes, contes et poésies*, *op. cit.*, p. 8.

[170]. *Cf.* LALOUETTE Claire, *Textes sacrés et Textes profanes de l'Ancienne Egypte*, volume 1: *op. cit.*, p. 142, p. 192, p. 266 and LALOUETTE Claire, *Textes sacrés et Textes profanes de l'Ancienne Egypte, volume II: Mythes, contes et poésies*, *op. cit.*, p. 34, p. 36, p. 125, p. 173.

[171]. For example for the text "la satire des métiers", translated by Claire LALOUETTE, *Textes sacrés et Textes profanes de l'Ancienne Egypte*, volume I: *Des Pharaons et des Hommes*, *op. cit.*, p.192; and for the *Coffin texts* translation by the same author, *op. cit.*, p. 266.

[172]. RACHET Guy, *Le livre des morts des anciens Égyptiens*, *op. cit.*, p.7, p. 41, p. 7, p. 41 on the Pyramids texts.

[173]. FRANKFORT Henri, *Ancient Egyptian Religion, An Interpretation, op. cit.*, p. 117.

[174]. GRIMAL Pierre, p. 6 of the preface to LALOUETTE Claire, *Textes sacrés et Textes profanes de l'ancienne Egypte*, tome 2, *op. cit.*

[175]. RACHET Guy, *Le livre des morts des anciens Égyptiens*, *op. cit.* , p. 141.

[176]. According to Claire LALOUETTE, *Textes sacrés et Textes profanes de l'Ancienne Egypte*, volume I: *op. cit.*, p. 84, translated from French: « Maât est la force de Rê, l'élu de Rê ».

[177]. RACHET Guy, *Le livre des morts des anciens Égyptiens,op. cit.*, p.174: "Je suis le maître de la lumière". (I am the master of light) p. 180 on light.

[178]. RACHET Guy, *Le livre des morts des anciens Égyptiens*, Editions du Rocher, 1996, p. 163.

[179]. *Cf.* "L'homme de l'Oasis" ("The peasant"), translation by Claire LALOUETTE, *Textes sacrés et Textes*

profanes de l'Ancienne Egypte, volume I: *Des Pharaons et des Hommes*, *op. cit.*, p. 203.

[180]. On the meaning of "righteous" and on the consequences of being in conformity with Maat, *cf.* FRANKFORT Henri, *Ancient Egyptian Religion, An Interpretation*, *op. cit.*, p. 72; *cf.* MORENZ Siegfried, *Egyptian Religion*, *op. cit.*, p. 113-116.

[181]. LALOUETTE Claire, *Textes sacrés et Textes profanes de l'Ancienne Egypte, volume II: Mythes, contes et poésies*, *op. cit.*, p. 32.

[182]. RACHET Guy, *Le livre des morts des anciens Égyptiens*, Editions du Rocher, 1996, p. 173-174 and p. 173.

[183]. On Maat and Isfet, *cf.* LICHTHEIM Myriam, *op. cit.*, p. 18.

[184]. RACHET Guy, *Le livre des morts des anciens Égyptiens*, *op. cit.*, p. 173-174 and p. 173.

[185]. YOYOTTE Jean, "Le jugement des morts selon l'Egypte ancienne", *op. cit.*, p. 21.

[186]. YOYOTTE Jean, "La pensée préphilosophique en Egypte", *op. cit.*, p. 1-23; p. 11.

[187]. FRANKFORT Henri, *Ancient Egyptian Religion, An Interpretation,op. cit.*, p. 132.

[188]. HORNUNG Erik, *L'esprit du temps des pharaons*, *op. cit.*, p. 99. Compare with "La prophéthie de Neferty" ("the Prophecy of Neferti"), translated by LALOUETTE Claire, *Textes sacrés et Textes profanes de l'Ancienne*

Egypte, volume I: *Des Pharaons et des Hommes*, *op. cit.*, p. 71.

[189]. HORNUNG Erik, *L'esprit du temps des pharaons*, *op. cit.*, p. 139.

[190]. LALOUETTE Claire, *Textes sacrés et Textes profanes de l'Ancienne Egypte, volume II: Mythes, contes et poésies*, *op. cit.*, p. 14.

[191]. RACHET Guy, *Le livre des morts des anciens Égyptiens*, *op. cit.*, p.145; compare with FAULKNER Raymond, *The Ancient Egyptian Book Of The Dead*, British Museum Press, London, 1996, p.79.

[192]. RACHET Guy, *Le livre des morts des anciens Égyptiens*, *op. cit.*, p. 151

[193]. RACHET Guy, *Le livre des morts des anciens Égyptiens*, *op. cit.*, p. 149.

[194]. RACHET Guy, *Le livre des morts des anciens Égyptiens*, *op. cit.*, p. 151.

[195]. Guy RACHET, *Le livre des morts des anciens Égyptiens*, *op. cit.*, p. 141.

[196]. RACHET Guy, *Le livre des morts des anciens Égyptiens*, *op. cit*.

[197]. "L'art de Vivre du Vizir Ptahhotep", translation by Claire LALOUETTE, *Textes sacrés et Textes profanes de l'Ancienne Egypte*, volume I: *Des Pharaons et des Hommes*, *op. cit.*, p. 241.

[198]. *Cf.* "LES DEUX SERPENTS DU REVE DE TANOUTAMON ET LA CONQUETE DE L'EGYPTE",

translation by LALOUETTE Claire, *Textes sacrés et Textes profanes de l'Ancienne Egypte*, volume I: *Des Pharaons et des Hommes*, *op. cit.*, p. 42.

[199]. L'art de Vivre du Vizir Ptahhotep", translation by Claire LALOUETTE, *Textes sacrés et Textes profanes de l'Ancienne Egypte*, volume I: *Des Pharaons et des Hommes*, *op. cit.*, p. 239.

[200]. *Cf.* "le Grand-prêtre Petosiris et sa famille (vers 360 av. JC)", translation by Claire LALOUETTE, *Textes sacrés et Textes profanes de l'Ancienne Egypte*, volume I: *Des Pharaons et des Hommes*, 1984, Gallimard/Unesco, p 262. *Cf.* on the heart as a guide, Myriam LICHTEHEIM, *op. cit.*, p. 53.

[201]. "L'art de Vivre du Vizir Ptahhotep", translation by Claire LALOUETTE, *Textes sacrés et Textes profanes de l'Ancienne Egypte*, volume I: *Des Pharaons et des Hommes*, 1984, Gallimard/Unesco, p. 236; and volume 2, p. 49.

[202]. *Cf.* "LES CHANTS DU DÉSESPÉRÉ XIIE DYNASTIE DIALOGUE ENTRE L'HOMME ET SON BA" translation by Claire LALOUETTE, *Textes sacrés et Textes profanes de l'Ancienne Egypte*, volume I: *Des Pharaons et des Hommes*, *op. cit.*, p. 222.

[203]. RACHET Guy, *Le livre des morts des anciens Egyptiens*, *op. cit.*, p. 61.

[204]. *Cf*: l' "ENSEIGNEMENT DU ROI AMENEMHAT I A SON FILS SESOSTRIS", translation by Claire

LALOUETTE, *Textes sacrés et Textes profanes de l'Ancienne Egypte*, volume I: Des Pharaons et des Hommes, 1984, Gallimard/Unesco, p. 57.

[205]. *Cf*: "Les lamentations d'IPOU-OUR", translation by Claire LALOUETTE, *Textes sacrés et Textes profanes de l'Ancienne Egypte*, volume I: *op. cit.*, p. 215.

[206]. *Cf* a book totally dedicated to this subject: PIANKOFF Alexandre, *Le "coeur" dans les textes égyptiens*, Paris, Librairie Paul Geuthner, 1930.

[207]. "LE DÉCRET D'HOREMHEB 1340 av JC", translation by LALOUETTE Claire, *Textes sacrés et Textes profanes de l'Ancienne Egypte*, volume I: *Des Pharaons et des Hommes*, *op. cit.*, p. 83.

[208]. SHUPAK Nili, "Some Idioms Connected With The Concept Of 'Heart'" in *Egypt And The Bible*, *Pharaonic Egypt, The Bible And Christianity*, Jerusalem, edition. S. Israelit-Groll, the Magnes Press, The Hebrew University, 1985, 202-212, p. 203 on the link between ears and the heart.

[209]. HORNUNG Erik, *L'esprit du temps des pharaons*, *op. cit.*, p. 134.

[210]. "La prophétie de Neferty", translation by LALOUETTE Claire, *Textes sacrés et Textes profanes de l'Ancienne Egypte*, volume I: *Des Pharaons et des Hommes*, *op. cit.*, p. 71.

[211]. RACHET Guy, *Le livre des morts des anciens Égyptiens*, *op. cit.*, p. 141; 149. *Cf.* also: "Textes sculptés

sur les parois d'une des chapelles de TOUTANKHAMON qui régna vers 1350 av. J-C ", translated by LALOUETTE Claire, textes sacrés, volume 1, *op. cit.*, p. 155 and same author same book p. 179: "LES EXPLOITS VALEUREUX DU COMMANDANT AMENEMHEB (vers 1480- 1440 av. J.-C.)".

[212]. RACHET Guy, *Le livre des morts des anciens Égyptiens*, *op. cit.*, p. 162-16; *cf.* also: "les Enseignements de Ptahotep", translation by LALOUETTE Claire, *Textes sacrés et Textes profanes de l'Ancienne Egypte*, volume I: *Des Pharaons et des Hommes*, 1984, Gallimard/Unesco, p. 265.

[213]. Which is a simple use of the principle of passage or not of an energy through a material thing.

[214]. RACHET Guy, *Le livre des morts des anciens Égyptiens*, *op. cit.*, p. 161.

[215]. RACHET Guy, *Le livre des morts des anciens Égyptiens*, *op. cit.*, p. 161.

[216]. "La satire des métiers", translation by Claire LALOUETTE, *Textes sacrés et Textes profanes de l'Ancienne Egypte*, volume I: *Des Pharaons et des Hommes*, *op. cit.*, p. 197; *cf* also "L'homme de l'Oasis", *ibid.*, p. 203; *ibid.*, p. 255 "l'enseignement du scribe Ani".

[217]. *Cf.* PIERRET, *Etudes Egyptologiques*, II, p. 94 ss, quoted by MORET Alexandre, "Rituel du culte divin en Egypte", p. 149, note n° 1.

[218]. We can find it in the *Book Of The Dead* regarding the deceased and in many texts regarding the Kings. *Cf.* for example: Claire LALOUETTE, *Textes sacrés et Textes profanes de l'Ancienne Egypte*, volume I: *Des Pharaons et des Hommes*, 1984, Gallimard/Unesco, p. 153 and p. 179.

[219]. LALOUETTE Claire, Textes sacrés et Textes profanes de l'Ancienne Egypte*, volume II: Mythes, contes et poésies*, 1987, *op. cit.*, p. 27.

[220]. "L'homme de l'Oasis", translation by Claire LALOUETTE, *Textes sacrés et Textes profanes de l'Ancienne Egypte*, volume I: *Des Pharaons et des Hommes*, 1984, Gallimard/Unesco, p. 204; and *ibid.,* p. 208, p. 209. *Cf.* LICHTHEIM Myriam, *op. cit.,* p. 59 "I abominate rapacity" and p. 61: "I am truly straight, free of greed".

[221]. On the lack of the concept of sin in Ancient Egypt: *cf.* FRANKFORT Henri, *Ancient Egyptian Religion, An Interpretation*, *op. cit.*, p. 73.

[222]. LALOUETTE Claire, *Textes sacrés et Textes profanes de l'Ancienne Egypte*, volume 1, *op. cit.*, p. 210.

[223]. *Cf.* Ani's papyrus, translated par Guy RACHET, *Le livre des morts des anciens Égyptiens*, *op. cit.*, p. 193.

[224]. "L'homme de l'Oasis", translation by Claire LALOUETTE, *Textes sacrés et Textes profanes de l'Ancienne Egypte*, volume I: *Des Pharaons et des Hommes*, *op. cit.*, p. 204.

[225]. "l'homme de l'Oasis", translation by Claire LALOUETTE, *Textes sacrés et Textes profanes de l'Ancienne Egypte*, volume I: *Des Pharaons et des Hommes*, 1984, Gallimard/Unesco, p. 205.

[226]. "L'INSTRUCTION ROYALISTE DE SEHETEPIBRÊ", translation by Claire LALOUETTE, *Textes sacrés et Textes profanes de l'Ancienne Egypte*, volume I: *Des Pharaons et des Hommes*, 1984, Gallimard/Unesco, p. 75.

[227]. RACHET Guy, *Le livre des morts des anciens Égyptiens*, *op. cit.*, p. 182.

[228]. "DIALOGUE ENTRE L'HOMME ET SON BA", translation by Claire LALOUETTE, *Textes sacrés et Textes profanes de l'Ancienne Egypte*, volume I: *Des Pharaons et des Hommes*, *op. cit.*, p. 225; comp. with the opinion of MORENZ on the meaning of the following hieroglyph of Maat: , MORENZ Siegfried, *Egyptian Religion*, *op. cit.*, p. 113 on the word "right".

[229]. RACHET Guy, *op. cit.*, p. 65, for an example of straight heart in relation to scales.

[230]. RACHET Guy, *Le livre des morts des anciens Égyptiens*, *op. cit.*, p. 141.

[231]. The modern concept of religion implies an adhesion to doctrines one cannot experiment. While in Ancient Egypt anyone could through ones senses and through ones physical and psychical states verify the functioning of Maat.

[232]. Many Egyptian texts speak about the physical rejuvenation, the prosperous life and the good health permitted by solar energy. On the contrary a lack of solar energy, due to a bad "hearing" of life results in body weakness, destruction of life, death. *cf.* LALOUETTE Claire, *Textes sacrés et Textes profanes de l'Ancienne Egypte*, volume I: *Des Pharaons et des Hommes*, *op. cit.*, p. 241; p. 75; p. 248 and p. 205.

[233]. *Cf.* "ENSEIGNEMENT DU ROI KHETI III A SON FILS MERIKARÊ", translation by Claire LALOUETTE, *Textes sacrés et Textes profanes de l'Ancienne Egypte*, volume I: *Des Pharaons et des Hommes*, 1984, Gallimard/Unesco, p. 52.

[234]. RACHET Guy, *Le livre des morts des anciens Égyptiens*, *op. cit.*, p. 86.

[235]. It is also stated that it is linked to the free flow of the water of the Nile, during the inundations. But these last are also due to a cosmic phenomenon as the Sirius star announces the Nile inundations. On this cosmic phenomenon, *Cf.* WILSON Hilary, *Understanding Hieroglyphs*, London, Brockhampton Press, 1999, p. 174.

[236]. SHIRUN-GRUMACH Irene, "Remarks On The Goddess MAAT", *Pharaonic Egypt, The Bible And Christianity*, *op. cit.*, p. 173 on the feather, Maat, and the light.

[237]. *Op. cit.*, p. 29 and note 10, translated from French "Puisse-t-il vivre, être en bonne santé et prospérer". *Cf.* also

---

LICHTHEIM Myriam, *op. cit.,* p. 27 "life, prosperity, health!".

[238]. Translation by Claire LALOUETTE, *Textes sacrés et Textes profanes de l'Ancienne Egypte*, volume I: *Des Pharaons et des Hommes*, 1984, Gallimard/Unesco p. 29, p. 33, p. 67, p. 239, p. 258, and p. 75: "Enseignements à Mérikarê".

[239]. As an example, *cf.* LICHTHEIM Myriam, *op. cit.,* p. 35: "I am a hearer who hears the truth, I am exact like the balance, truly straight like Thoth". On filling the ears with Maat, *cf.;* LICHTHEIM Myriam, *op. cit.*, p. 50 "who fills the ears of Horus with truth".

[240]. Claire LALOUETTE, *Textes sacrés et Textes profanes de l'Ancienne Egypte*, volume I: *Des Pharaons et des Hommes*, 1984, Gallimard/Unesco, p. 37, p. 67; p. 92, p. 152, p. 155, p. 184.

[241]. On justice as the art of sharing *cf.* previous note n° 199.

BIBLIOGRAPHY

AMÉLINEAU Emile, *La morale égyptienne quinze siècles avant notre ère, Etude sur le papyrus de Boulaq n° 4*, Paris, Editions Ernest Leroux, 1892

ASSMANN Jan, *Maât, l'Egypte pharaonique et l'idée de justice sociale*, Conférences essais et leçons du Collège de France, Paris, Julliard, 1989

BICKEL S., *La cosmogonie égyptienne avant le Nouvel Empire*, Fribourg, 1999

BLEEKER Claas Jouco, *De Beteekenis van de Egyptische Godin Ma-a-t*, Leiden, 1929

BLEEKER Claas Jouco, *Egyptians Festivals, Enactments Of Religious Renewal*, Leiden, Netherlands, E.J. Brill, 1967

BLEIBERG Edward, *The official Gift In Ancient Egypt*, Oklahoma, University of Oklahoma Press. 1996

CHAMPOLLION, *L'Egypte de Jean-François CHAMPOLLION*, ouvrage collectif, Paris, Mengès, 1998

DERCHAIN Philippe, *Le papyrus Salt 825 (BM 10051) rituel pour la conservation de la vie en Egypte*, Bruxelles, Académie royale de Belgique, Mémoire n° 1784, Classe des lettres, volume LVIII, fasc. I a, 1965

DRIOTON Etienne, "Le jugement des âmes dans l'Egypte ancienne", Revue du Caire, 1949, p. 1-20

FAULKNER R.O., *The Ancient Egyptian Book Of The Dead*, London, British Museum, 1996

FRANKFORT H, FRANKFORT A, WILSON, JACOBSON AND IRWIN, *The Intellectual Adventure Of Ancient Man*, Chicago, University of Chicago Press, 1946

FRANKFORT Henri, *Ancient Egyptian Religion, An Interpretation*, New York, Columbia University Press, 1948

FRANKFORT Henri, *Kingship And The Gods*, Chicago, 1948

GOFF Beatrice L., *Symbols Of Ancient Egypt In The Late Period, The Twenty-first Dynasty*, Yale University, Mouton publishers, 1979

GOYON Jean-Claude, *Maât et Pharaon ou le destin de l'Egypte antique*, Lyon, Editions ACV, 1998

GRIMAL Pierre, in Claire LALOUETTE, *Textes sacrés et Textes profanes de l'Ancienne Egypte*, volume I, *Des Pharaons et des Hommes*, 1984, Gallimard/Unesco, p. 8 and p. 16

HERODOTE, *L'Enquête*, Book I to IV, édition d'Andrée BARQUET, Paris, Gallimard, Folio classique, 1964

HORNUNG Erik, *L'esprit du temps des pharaons*, Paris, Hachette, collection Pluriel, 1996

IVERSEN Erik, *The Myth Of Egypt And Its Hieroglyphs in European Tradition*, Copenhagen, GEC Gad, 1961

LALOUETTE Claire, *Textes sacrés et Textes profanes de l'Ancienne Egypte*, volume I : *Des Pharaons et des Hommes*, Paris, Gallimard/Unesco, 1984

LALOUETTE Claire, *Textes sacrés et Textes profanes de l'Ancienne Egypte, volume II : Mythes, contes et poésies*, Paris, Gallimard/Unesco, 1987

LICHTHEIM Myriam, *Maat In Egyptian Autobiographies And Related Studies*, Fribourg, Universitätsverlag Freiburg

Schweiz, Vandenthoeck and Ruprecht Göttingen, 1992

MENU Bernadette, "Le tombeau de Pétosiris (2) Maât, Thot et le droit", Paris, BIFAO (Bulletin de l'Institut Français d'Archéologie Orientale), t. 95 (1995), p. 281-295

MORENZ Siegfried, *Egyptian Religion*, London, Methuen and Co litd, 1976

MORET Alexandre, "La doctrine de Maât", Revue d'Egyptologie, volume 4, Imprimerie de l'Institut français d'Archéologie Orientale, Le Caire, 1940, p. 1-14

MORET Alexandre, "Le jugement des morts, en Egypte et hors d'Egypte", Paris, Annales du Musée GUIMET, volume XXXII, p. 255-287

MORET Alexandre, *Le Nil et la civilisation égyptienne*, Paris, La Renaissance du livre, 1926

MORET Alexandre, *Rituel du culte divin journalier en Egypte*, Paris, Ernest Leroux, 1902

PIANKOFF Alexandre, *Le "coeur" dans les textes égyptiens*, Paris, Librairie Paul Geuthner, 1930

RACHET Guy, *Le livre des morts des anciens Égyptiens*, Paris, Editions du Rocher, 1996

REVILLOUT Eugène, *Les origines égyptiennes du droit civil romain*, Paris, Librairie Paul Geuthner, 1912

SARRAF Joseph, *La notion du droit d'après les Anciens Egyptiens*, Rome, Città del Vaticano, Libreria editrice vaticana, 1984, Collana storia e attualità, No 10

SHAW Ian and NICHOLSON Paul, *Dictionary Of Ancient Egypt*, London, British Museum Press, 1995

SHIRUN-GRUMACH Irene, "Remarks on the Goddess MAAT", *Pharaonic Egypt, The Bible And Christianity*, Jerusalem, ed. S. Israelit-Groll, the Magnes Press, The Hebrew University, 1985, 173-201

SHUPAK Nili, "Some idioms connected with the concept of 'heart' in Egypt and the Bible", *Pharaonic Egypt, The Bible And Christianity*, Jerusalem, éd. S. Israelit-Groll, the Magnes Press, The Hebrew University, 1985, 202-212

TEETER Emily, *The Presentation Of Maat, Ritual and Legitimacy in Ancient Egypt,* Chicago, The University of Chicago, 1997

WILSON Hilary, *Understanding Hieroglyphs*, London, Brockhampton Press, 1999

YOYOTTE Jean, Entretien avec, "L'échange est au coeur de la civilisation égyptienne", *Eurêka*, Paris, BAYARD PRESSE, Septembre 1998, n° 35

YOYOTTE Jean, "La pensée préphilosophique en Egypte", extr. Encyclopédie de la Pléiade, histoire de la philosophie, I, Paris 19.., p.1-23

YOYOTTE Jean, "Le jugement des morts selon l'Egypte ancienne", Paris, Sources Orientales, IV, 1961, p. 17-71

Also by Anna MANCINI:

ANCIENT ROMAN SOLUTIONS TO MODERN LEGAL ISSUES

The Example of Patent Law

Our Law and its philosophy have been conceived for an economic world where the main source of wealth was material. Although this world no longer exists, its laws are still alive and slow down the development of modern economies. Patent law strikingly shows this fact. Invented mainly during the industrial revolution in order to protect tangible inventions, it could not be applied to the new intangible inventions of the 20th century. Software, for example, has been denied protection under patent law, due to its lack of materiality. Since such a cause of denial is economically absurd, we should adapt patent law to the virtual world. This was not done and so no new intangible invention can benefit from this protection through a lack of tangibility. Long before us, the ancient Romans had understood that the intangible world and the material world do not function the same way. Since they were very practical people, they took this reality into account to build their legal system. Their legal experience has become valuable for a modern world that is rediscovering the value of ideas and people's wealth, too long eclipsed by materialism.

Anna MANCINI, Ph. D.

Categories: Law, Patent Law, Philosophy of Law, Roman Law

ISBN: 1-932848-04-5 (paperback)
ISBN: 1-932848-05-3 (E-book)

Available on WWW.BUENOSBOOKSAMERICA.COM

Other books in French and Spanish also available.

Printed in the United States
42006LVS00002B/15